PRAISE FOR
COACHING GIRLS' SOCCER

"*Coaching Girls' Soccer* provides the essential tools for creating an environment in which every player is given the best opportunity to hone her soccer skills and develop a lifetime desire to play the game. I highly recommend this book to all coaches who currently coach, or aspire to coach, girls' soccer."

—Jan Smisek, U.S. Soccer, National Staff Coach

"*Coaching Girls' Soccer* is a must read for the novice coach getting involved with a youth girls team, and an insightful guide for coaches of all experience levels."

—Lesle D. Gallimore, Head Women's Soccer Coach, University of Washington, and National Academy Staff Coach, National Soccer Coaches Association of America

"John DeWitt is recognized for his excellence in the development of players. Any work of his is a sure bet to enhance players' abilities and the joy that they encounter toward that pursuit."

—Tony DiCicco, Chief Operations Office, Women's United Soccer Association (WUSA); Head Coach, 1996 Olympic Gold Medalist and 1999 World Cup Champions

ALSO IN THE
COACHING GIRLS SERIES

Coaching Girls' Basketball
Sandy L. Simpson

Coaching Girls' Softball
Kathy Strahan

COACHING GIRLS' SOCCER

**From the How-To's of the Game to Practical
Real-World Advice—Your Definitive Guide
to Successfully Coaching Girls**

JOHN DEWITT

THREE RIVERS PRESS
NEW YORK

This book is dedicated to my wife, Janice,
who has supported me in every endeavor I attempt.

Published by Three Rivers Press, New York, New York.
Member of the Crown Publishing Group, a division of Random House, Inc.
www.randomhouse.com

THREE RIVERS PRESS and the Tugboat design are registered trademarks of Random House, Inc.

Originally published by Prima Publishing, Roseville, California, in 2001.

Illustrations by Pamela Tanzey and Andrew Vallas

Printed in the United States of America

Library of Congress Cataloging-in-Publication Data
DeWitt, John (John Kenneth).
    Coaching girls' soccer : from the how-to's of the game to practical real-world advice, your definitive guide to successfully coaching girls / John DeWitt.
        p. cm.
    Includes index.
    1. Soccer—Coaching.   2. Soccer for women.   I. Title.

GV943.8 D49 2001
796.334'07'7—dc21   2001033178

ISBN 0-7615-3249-8

10 9 8 7 6

First Edition

CONTENTS

INTRODUCTION

SOCCER. FOOTBALL. FUTBOL. Known by many different names in different countries around the world, soccer is by far the largest participation sport on Earth. According to Federation Internationale de Football Association (FIFA), the international governing body of the sport, more than 40 million females in more than 100 countries consider themselves to be soccer players. If you add to that the number of people who watch the game, you begin to realize the immensity of this sport's following.

In the United States alone, soccer's participation numbers rival that of any other organized sport. In 1995, with the United States Youth Soccer Association (USYSA), the American Youth Soccer Organization (AYSO), and the Soccer Association for Youth (SAY), there were more than 2,983,826 youth players on teams and in leagues across the country. In a report released by the Sporting Goods Manufacturers Association (SGMA), soccer was the "hot" team sport of the 1990s, with an 11 percent increase by the end of the decade. USYSA programs increased 76 percent during that time span. Why so many players?

- **Soccer is simple to play.** The object of the game is to get the ball into a goal. Only one player on each team, the goalkeeper, may use her hands, and only in an area called the penalty box in front of the goal being defended. The rest of the players may not use their hands or arms, but may use any other part of their bodies to move the ball.

- **Soccer can be played by just about anyone.** Unlike such sports as basketball and football, soccer does not require a specific body type or physical attribute for a player to be successful. Short or tall people, slow or fast people, small or big people—all can become exceptional players, because these different qualities are useful in different areas on the field. Boys and girls can play the game equally well, although as players get older, physical differences between males and females make it difficult for teams of different genders to compete at an equal level.

- **Soccer requires minimal equipment.** A soccer player's full gear includes shorts, a shirt, shin guards (made of hard plastic to protect against injuries from being kicked), and shoes. A ball and a goal are all that is needed to get a game going. An official field will be lined and have goal posts and a crossbar with a net attached, but you don't need all of that to play soccer. A game (or "match," as a soccer game is actually called) can be played with goals made from two markers, a duffel bag, a trash can, or just about anything.

- **Soccer games can be played outdoors or indoors.** Because soccer involves a minimum of equipment, it is easily adaptable to playing in a gymnasium or indoor soccer arena. In fact, because it is so simple to set up, a practice or game doesn't even have to be on a regulation field—it could be on an open space in a park or even on a beach.

- **Soccer is relatively inexpensive to play.** Although it is possible to pay a large amount of money for special training, uniforms, travel to tournaments, and training equipment, in theory, soccer is a very cheap sport. Chapter 4 talks about the extra things that money can buy, but for now, realize that the only required cost is the cost of a soccer ball. If you are in an organized league, there will be league fees and refereeing fees, and a fee for your daughter's uniform, but when compared with the costs of some other organized sports, soccer is relatively cheap.

THE LEVELS OF PLAY IN WOMEN'S SOCCER

The U.S. National Team established itself as one of the premier women's soccer teams on the planet when it won the Women's World Cup in 1999 with its penalty kick victory over China. Many of the players, such as Mia Hamm and Brandi Chastain, have become household names. More than 40 million people watched the game on television, and the Rose Bowl in Pasadena, California, was sold out, with more than 90,000 spectators witnessing the action. This figure broke all attendance records for a women's sporting event. The U.S.

National Team's 1999 World Cup gave a huge push to women's soccer, ensuring that it would be a sport supported by most of America.

In addition to the World Cup victory, Americans won the Silver Medal in the 2000 Sydney Olympics, the Gold Medal in the 1996 Atlanta Olympics, finished third in the 1995 Women's World Championships in Sweden, and were the World Champions in the 1991 World Championships in China. Perhaps the success of these teams has helped to increase girls' participation, or maybe the participation of girls has helped to increase the popularity of the team.

In the United States, there are a variety of levels of soccer play, ranging from the U.S. National Teams to professional leagues, to college teams, to youth groups. Opportunities for girls to participate at all levels have increased as we entered the new millennium. In the past, the United States sponsored one women's national team with few youth national teams. Currently U.S. Soccer not only fields the full national team (the one that won the World Cup), but also youth national teams at the U21, U19, and U16 age levels. Because there is no world championship yet established for the U21 and U16 teams, they participate in competitions with teams from other countries or with college, regional, or club teams within the United States. The U19 national team will participate in the first-ever U19 Women's World Youth Championship in Canada during August and September of 2002.

On the professional side, the Women's United Soccer Association (WUSA), the first full-time professional league for women's soccer, had its inaugural season in the spring of 2001. The league has full sponsorship and is the first opportunity for elite women to compete while making soccer a full-time job. There is also the United States Women's Interregional Soccer League (USWISL), which is a lower level pro league that has been around since the mid-1990s. The players in the USWISL may receive some compensation for their play, but not enough to make it their only job.

In college, sponsorship by universities in the National Collegiate Athletic Association (NCAA) and National Association of Intercollegiate Athletics (NAIA) has increased to more than 800 programs across the country. In 1981, there were only 77 schools that fielded varsity soccer teams. Players on university teams sometimes receive scholarships that pay for all or a part of their education—the amount varies according to the school's NCAA or NAIA division and the program's budget. Not all players on a university team receive athletic aid, but it is available at the discretion of the coach.

Players who are 19 or younger compete in what is termed "youth soccer." Players might play for their high school teams, which would be separate from their club teams. The difference is that a high school team is comprised of players who attend that high school, while a club team can be made up of anyone who meets the age requirement for a given team. Some leagues or state associations may have additional rules regarding eligibility. In addition, high school soccer occurs during a given season as mandated by the state high school athletic association, while club soccer may run year-round. According to the National Federation of State High School Associations, 270,273 girls competed for high school teams during the 1999–2000 school year. This is up from the 191,350 girls who played in 1995. It has been estimated by the Soccer Industry Council of America (SICA), that more than 7.4 million females played soccer at least once in 1999.

BENEFITS OF SPORTS FOR YOUNG GIRLS

Girls play sports because sports are fun. Girls derive enjoyment from their participation. As soon as playing ceases to be fun, girls tend to stop playing. But there are also other benefits of competing in organized sport that transfer to success in everyday life:

• **Self-discipline.** Players learn the importance of completing tasks that they might not otherwise do if they were not involved in sports—attending training sessions, paying attention at practices and games, and attending and being on time for other related activities.

• **Cooperation.** In any team sport, a vital ingredient of success is the ability to cooperate with others. In soccer, as in most sports, players in different positions have different responsibilities. Part of the beauty of soccer, however, is that when your team has the ball, everyone is on the attack, and when your team doesn't have the ball, everyone defends.

• **Selflessness.** You probably have heard the expression, "There is no *I* in team." Players in team sports have the chance to learn the important concept that a successful team requires individuals to make sacrifices. You can't have a soccer team without a goalkeeper, and it's tough to have a team with only 11 players, so that means that not everyone will play every minute.

• **Commitment.** An important issue in today's world involves following through with what you say you are going to do. A team can't function if only half the people show up to practice or games. Although the coach sets the rules and expectations for all team members, it is up to the individual players (and often their parents) to follow the guidelines.

- **Responsibility.** No matter the age of your players, participating on a team requires a demonstration of responsibility. Individuals are responsible for their equipment and for their actions. They are also responsible for letting the coach know if they will be unable to attend a training session or game.

As a coach, a major part of your job will be teaching these life skills to your players. Joining a team does not automatically instill these concepts—they must be learned. Some of your greatest triumphs, and also your biggest headaches, will come from the players' demonstration of or ignoring of these ideas. When I got into coaching, I made the mistake of thinking that a good coach is someone who can teach the game of soccer, but I have since come to realize that teaching soccer is only one aspect of coaching—teaching life skills is even more important.

MY EXPERIENCE AND CREDENTIALS

Why should you listen to me? I have been coaching soccer for the past 14 years at levels ranging from five-year-olds to adults. I have my A coaching license from the U.S. Soccer Federation, and I also possess the National Youth License, which is geared toward teaching coaches the specific needs of players 12 and under. Remember that the players are children—not little adults—and they must be treated accordingly. For the past 10 years I have coached primarily girl's teams, and have had the experience of working with college teams and select youth teams. One of my greatest memories was my experience in the observer program with the U.S. Women's National Team prior to the 1996 Olympics. I was able to spend a week at the team's training camp and witness firsthand the team meetings and training sessions that prepared the team to win the Gold Medal.

When I relocated to Arizona for graduate school in 1990, I decided that I wanted to get into coaching in my new state. I approached the coach of a boys' team to see if I could help. He directed me to the club president, who asked if I would be willing to work with a girls' team within the club. I had become a "drafted" coach. Although I had no experience with girls, I was eager to get into coaching, so I readily agreed. Since then I have worked primarily with girl's teams. While things change from level to level, the basic needs of females remain common, and I have learned a lot in the past ten years.

WHY ARE YOU READING THIS BOOK?

This book is intended to help you become better at coaching youth girls at soccer, and chances are that many of your players are having their first soccer experience. I am going to guess that you are involved in the game in one of the following four ways:

1. New volunteer coach. You have always enjoyed sports, and you have played organized sports in the past. You may have played soccer, or possibly this is your first experience in this sport. You became a coach because you wanted to. This is how I got into coaching back when I was still in college.

2. New drafted coach. With the great increases over the past few years in the number of girls playing, the need for coaches has also increased. You took your daughter to sign up for a team or league, and when you arrived you were told a coach was needed. You might have been pressured to become the coach because no one else would "volunteer." You were drafted.

3. Experienced coach looking for new ideas. You have been coaching soccer for a while, but you are always on the lookout for new ideas. This might be your first time coaching girls. I live by the philosophy that good coaches are good thieves—we are always looking to find new ideas to incorporate into our coaching arsenal. Sometimes presenting a skill or concept in a different way helps players to understand it more easily, and you are on the lookout for different games or exercises to help with your team.

4. Parent of athlete. Your daughter is playing soccer or you are thinking about getting your daughter involved, but you have little experience in the game. You hope to increase your knowledge about soccer so you can enjoy games and practices more.

No matter which category you fall into, this book will help you. Not only will you learn more about coaching girls, but you will also get practical advice on games, practice sessions, and typical issues that arise in youth soccer.

WHAT CAN YOU EXPECT FROM THIS BOOK?

This book has been designed to help coaches who work with 7- to 13-year-old girls to become better at their task and to improve as coaches. Although the book is intended for newer coaches, experienced coaches will be able to gain ideas and insights too. Some of the topics that will be discussed include:

- Methods used by successful coaches: Little things that make great coaches.
- Differences between boys and girls: Train the athlete, but keep the gender in mind.
- Practice planning: How to set up and administer a successful training session.
- Techniques: How to perform and teach soccer's fundamental skills.
- Soccer strategies: How to teach your players to score goals and to keep the opposition from scoring.
- Team management: You've got a team—now what?

It is my hope that this book will help you find greater enjoyment in your involvement in soccer. While not every idea, game, or strategy may apply to your team, I hope that by reading this book you become better at teaching the greatest game on Earth!

1

So You Want to Be a Coach

COACHING A SPORT CAN be a very rewarding and satisfying endeavor. Coaching provides an opportunity to work with young people to help them master difficult skills, learn the concepts of teamwork and responsibility, and improve their self-esteem. Coaching also gives you chances to learn about yourself. The task that all coaches face is to provide athletes with opportunities to improve their skills in an environment that can be both frustrating and challenging. In any league, tournament, or competition, there is one winner and usually many disappointed teams. While you will get plenty of chances to experience the elation of winning, you will probably also have opportunities to deal with the frustration of defeat. It is my experience that when all is taken into account, the positives outweigh the negatives. I hope that the same can be said for you.

THE ROLE OF THE COACH

It is easy to think that the sole role of a coach is to run practices and then stand on the sidelines during games while making substitutions, calling out advice, and determining how the team should play the game. These are only a few of the coach's duties, however. The coach also has to perform a variety of roles, many of which might not be apparent at first. As players grow older, the coach's role can change, moving from facilitator when the players are young to teacher when the players develop and are capable of understanding and performing more advanced tasks. The most important thing to remember is that without players, there are no coaches. The athletes that we work with are the reason we have our jobs, and we are there to serve them.

To be a successful soccer coach, you must have practical knowledge about soccer. Your knowledge base does not have to be extensive, but you must at least have an understanding of the rules of the game, how to execute basic techniques correctly, and an understanding of basic strategies. Future chapters will help you to grasp and increase your knowledge about these concepts.

Knowing how to play the game, however, does not guarantee success as a coach. There are other roles that you will fill when coaching young people. Obviously, you need to be capable of communicating your knowledge to your team. You need to be able to teach. You need to be a facilitator to help guide and enhance your players' performance. You will be a manager of equipment and people, and you will have to be effective at administering your team. It is also probable that you will need to act as a fundraiser, recruiter, and trainer. In short, you will need to wear many hats as a coach, and your job will require much more than knowing your X's and O's.

The Coach Is a Teacher

The most important role of the coach is that of teacher. A teacher prepares students for a certain task or test. In this case, the subject matter is the fundamentals of soccer, and the test is the game. Topics include how to perform skills correctly (technique), how to make correct decisions during the game (tactics), how to be in good physical condition (fitness), and how to cooperate with teammates (psychology). No matter which area you choose to focus on during a given lesson, it is important to remember that your job is to teach your athletes, just as if you were in a classroom.

While choosing what you will teach to your players, it helps to have an understanding about how a person learns. Repetition, or repeating an action over and over until it becomes natural, is the key to mastering a skill. Practice does not necessar-

Coaching Tip

Coaches fill many roles. In each role, the coach is a role model. As a teacher, the coach models the many aspects of the game. As a facilitator, the coach models how to interact with others. As a person, the coach models good sportsmanship and respect for others.

THE GAME IS THE BEST TEACHER

Many times during coaching clinics or when learning about soccer, the first thing a coach asks is, "What is the best way to teach my players the game?" The answer is very simple, yet it is often not what new coaches want or expect to hear. There is no magic exercise or special activity that teaches soccer better than the game itself. The best coaches use playing as their primary method of teaching. Soccer is a player's game—a game in which the players must be able to make decisions and act quickly. There are no time outs, and play is continuous (except of course when the ball goes out of bounds). Much of the instruction given during games must be processed immediately, and very often the athletes are not able to make immediate changes while trying to play. Therefore, the best time for coaching comes during practices, not during games. Before games, at halftime, and when players are on the bench, you can offer advice, but you cannot stop play to do so.

ily make perfect, but it does make permanent. Incorrect repetition will only make your players better at performing skills incorrectly. Therefore, you need to know how skills are carried out accurately in order to help your team realize their mistakes and understand how to correct them.

The Coach Is a Role Model

While working with young girls, you will be one of their role models in just about all aspects of life. Like it or not, you will have a great influence upon your players. How you carry yourself, how you react to situations, and how you communicate will serve as examples to them of how to properly behave. You are an adult, and you will have as much impact on their beliefs as do their parents and schoolteachers. You need to keep this in mind at all times because remarks or actions that you are not even thinking about form lasting impressions upon your players and their parents.

If you attend a soccer game during which the parents and players seem rowdy, take a look at the coach. Chances are that the coach is leading the pack, even though he or she might not mean to. Because your players and their parents will look to you and your behavior, you must conduct yourself responsibly at all times. If you consistently arrive late for practices and games, expect your players to do the same. Your actions will make much more of an impression than your words.

The Coach Is a Facilitator

A facilitator is a person who makes performance or play less difficult. Unlike a teacher, a facilitator might not be concerned with the concepts of learning, but rather sets up environments in which the players perform, play for the sake of playing, and learn on their own. Because of the cognitive abilities of young players (eight years and under), their coaches often are more or less facilitators. This does not mean that there is not any teaching. Instead, a bulk of the coaching should be spent organizing activities or exercises and letting the girls learn on their own. In most successful practices, you will be a teacher at some times and a facilitator at others. Teaching might be completed early in the practice and facilitation near the end, or the teaching and facilitating may alternate as training progresses. Players learn the most while doing, not while listening. Therefore, an effective coach is both a teacher and a facilitator.

The Coach Is an Equipment Manager

You are going to need equipment to run training sessions and to organize the team. Some equipment—such as game uniforms, shin guards, and shoes—will be needed by each girl. Even though each player will probably purchase her own shoes and shin guards, you might be asked for your opinion about what they should buy. Some teams choose to get additional gear, like duffel bags, sweatshirts, or training suits. Check with your league—uniforms are sometimes provided by the league or club, or perhaps there is a specific uniform style, brand, or color that is required by your club. If not, you might have to arrange for the ordering of, payment for, and lettering of your team's uniforms.

In addition to uniforms, you must also have equipment to help you run training sessions. These items include cones or disks for field markings, vests or practice jerseys to use when dividing the group into teams, soccer balls, and perhaps a soccer net. Some coaches also purchase teaching aids like clipboards or magnetic boards. These are good for diagramming plays and positions for the girls. Other coaches own portable soccer goals that can be easily transported to and from training and assembled quickly.

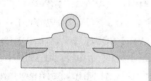

Coaching Tip

Require players to wear white shirts to practice and to carry a dark shirt in their duffel bags. That way you don't have to purchase practice bibs for dividing girls into identifiable practice groups.

WHAT KIND OF SHOES SHOULD I BUY?

There are many different styles and types of shoes that are appropriate for players. Encourage parents to purchase shoes that fit correctly. Shoes in soccer are as important as a glove is in baseball, and correct fit is critical for both injury prevention and proper learning of skills. Local used sporting goods shops are good places to look for shoes that are still in good condition. They are also great places to take shoes once the girls grow out of them.

There are three basic styles of soccer shoe:

1. *Flats* are exactly what their name implies: flat-soled shoes with no cleats or studs. They are suitable on artificial turf, indoors, and in locations where the ground is hard. Running and tennis shoes are flats, and many shoe manufacturers have at least one style in their soccer lines.

2. *Molded cleats* are probably the most common shoes used in soccer. They have molded bumps on the sole that are used to increase traction. Molded cleats are appropriate outdoors on grassy fields. The cleats are not removable.

3. *Screw-ins* are cleated shoes with removable and replaceable cleats. The cleats are usually longer than those found on molded shoes. This shoe is appropriate for older players on very soft or wet fields.

For younger players, a pair of molded cleats or flats is probably the most appropriate.

The Coach Is an Administrator

In most soccer organizations, clubs, and leagues, there is a lot of paperwork: registration forms, injury waivers, players' passes, and other required information. If your team is going to participate in tournaments, entry forms need to be completed. Usually a roster and formal application must be filled out and submitted, and if the tournament is out of state, additional travel forms might be necessary. This can become quite tasking and time-consuming, but it is a part of the functioning of the team. Although most paperwork will be completed before the season begins, you could find yourself spending your free time filling out forms. Get a binder to help with your organization.

The Coach Is a Manager

A manager is a person who is in charge of individuals, groups, or items. As discussed earlier, your role as an equipment manager is to be in charge of the team's equipment. You will also have to manage people—yourself, your assistants, your players, and their parents. This will require discipline, tact, and effective communication skills. It is much easier to find successful coaches with average knowledge who can manage well than it is to find successful coaches who possess great technical knowledge but cannot manage. When coaching young people, common sense will usually dictate your proper course of action, but there will be many times when you will be challenged. Reflection prior to action is a good course to take. The ability to manage well also requires that you can identify with the other person, whether it be player or parent, and see things from his or her point of view. You need to be flexible and allow for different points of view.

The Coach Is a Fundraiser or Treasurer

Running a team costs money. In addition to league fees and uniform costs, teams need finances to pay for tournaments and travel, to purchase equipment, and to pay for miscellaneous expenses as they occur. Many teams enjoy having a preseason or end of season party to enjoy each other's company and to bring things to a close. There are many ways to accomplish this with little or no cost, but if your team would like to have a party at a local pizza or ice cream parlor, or if you would like to hand out awards, you need to spend money. For a youth team, most of these expenses are very small, and a donation from each family or a local sponsor can defray costs. However, if you decide that your team will attend tournaments, especially those involving travel, or if you decide that you would like to have a guest expert coach work with the group, the cost of participating can increase dramatically. It is not uncommon for teams to run fundraisers, such as car washes, bake sales, and other activities, to earn the needed money. If this is the case, the activities will need to be monitored and the money will have to be managed. Many teams set up a special checking account so the account can be drawn upon to pay required expenses.

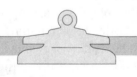

Coaching Tip

The role of treasurer is a perfect task for a parent to take on. In fact, I would highly recommend handing this off to another trustworthy person to save yourself from potential headaches.

The Coach Is a Recruiter

As you continue coaching from season to season, you will find that there is turnover among the members of your team. This happens no matter how hard you try to provide players with opportunities to improve in an environment that they enjoy. Some players will move away, leave to join other teams, or decide not to continue playing soccer. Because there will always be turnover, coaches are required to encourage potential players to join their teams. Though it is unethical to break any league, club, or state organization rules when looking for potential players, it is highly probable that you will be approached by a player or parent with a request to join your team. At this point, assuming that you would like the player to join, you become a recruiter.

Unfortunately a pervasive attitude exists in sports today that places an unhealthy emphasis on winning over player development. Many times recruiting battles occur over ten-year-olds that rival those of collegiate recruiting. It is too bad that some young girls will be denied opportunities to play because their coach has decided that he or she would like to have a better player on the team. Keep in mind your reasons for coaching. Your priority must place the welfare of the players ahead of your own. If you need to recruit players because you have openings on your team, be sure to conduct yourself in a manner that is ethical and reasonable. You should not approach players who play for another team. Instead, advertise your tryouts and respond to any inquiries.

You may also find yourself on the other side of the situation, coaching players who are being recruited by another coach. If this occurs, I would advise that you do the following:

1. Check your league or state rules concerning coaches contacting players. If the other coach is breaking a rule, report him or her to the proper league authorities. This could create some uncomfortable situations, but it is the proper way to address the issue.

2. If the other coach is following league rules, speak with the parents of the recruited player. If she is considering leaving your

DELEGATION IS IMPORTANT

When you think of all the duties and tasks that must be completed to successfully run a team of any age group, you may find that it could be a full-time job. One of the best ways to keep yourself from going crazy is to delegate duties to assistant coaches, or better yet, to the parents of the players on your team. For example, a parent who has the job of Uniform Manager can coordinate uniform purchases. If your league meetings require that a team representative attend, but it does not have to be you, a parent could be the Team Rep and attend for you. This is a great way to get parents involved with the team as more than just spectators or potential problems.

team, and you would like her to stay, ask her why she is considering leaving. Be non-confrontational, and listen to what they say. If they give reasons that are plausible and realistic, let them go. If they tell you about the benefits of playing on another team and in reality they receive those same benefits on your team, remind them of that. It is easy to think that things are better elsewhere.

3. Eliminate the situation before it begins. By coaching effectively, make your team a team that everyone wants to play on. Create an atmosphere that you would like to play in, and treat your players the way that you would like to be treated. Sounds simple, but it is easy to overlook, and it is an effective way to make yourself better as a coach.

The Coach Is an Athletic Trainer and Physical Therapist

Unless your team or organization provides a full-time athletic training staff that is accessible to all players on your team, many times you will be looked upon to act as a trainer to help treat injuries. It is important to have a basic knowledge of first aid and minor injury treatment, but also to be very conservative whenever giving feedback about an injury. Any head injuries or injuries that are not obvious should be referred to a hospital or emergency room. There is only one thing that can verify if a bone has been broken: an x ray. Most injuries that occur to young people are minor in nature, and require only bandages or ice. Because you are the person who works directly with the players, the girls and their parents will often look to you for you advice on these matters.

YOUR COACHING STYLE AND PHILOSOPHY

Your coaching style is the manner in which you work with the players and parents on your team. Many different styles of coaching are successful, depending on the coach. The style that works best for you is the one that comes naturally. So be yourself, and you'll find your style. Over time, you may change as you gain more experience. You may find that there is a certain style that your players respond to better than others. Many successful coaches have employed very different styles.

Your coaching philosophy is the set of beliefs that guide you as you coach and administer your team. Many of your philosophies will come from your personal experience. You might have developed these beliefs because of influences that your coaches had on you, whether positive or negative. I have played and worked with coaches whom I have tried to emulate. There are also people who have acted in ways that I do not want to replicate. It is important that before you enter into coaching, you think about your coaching philosophy, because it will dictate your course of action. It is also important that once you come up with your philosophy, you express it to your players and their parents, because it directly affects them. Many times sharing your philosophy can eliminate potential problems because the others know where you are coming from. It can also eliminate problems because individuals may choose not be a part of your team if they do not adhere to your philosophies. This is okay—you are better off without them. You will not be able to make everyone happy.

The Three Coaching Styles

One can characterize coaching styles in many different ways, but I think that there are three main styles: authoritarian, chief executive officer (CEO), and friend. Any coach's style can be identified either as one of the three distinct styles or as some combination of two or all three. Many coaches employ each of the three styles at different times in order to motivate their players.

An *authoritarian coach* makes all the decisions for the team. There is little or no room for questioning, and the players must complete every task the coach assigns. The coach is the boss, and it is his or her role to tell the athletes what to do. It is the athlete's role to listen, absorb, and perform. There are times when an authoritarian approach is necessary and desirable, such as when a new skill is being introduced or when the team is having trouble concentrating. The authoritarian coach has firm beliefs on how things should be done and expects players to conform. Many authoritarian coaches have enjoyed success using a particular method or approach and believe that there is no need to try other methods or playing styles.

The *CEO coach* is one who runs his or her team as if it were a corporation. The bottom line for the CEO coach is production, and production is determined by the coach's philosophy. The CEO coach is very flexible. The CEO is willing to try new and different methods to increase or enhance productivity, but he or she will always be the person making the final decision. It is not uncommon for a CEO coach to ask for suggestions from colleagues or players. The CEO approach works well when you want to give players the opportunity to feel empowered and to be a part of the decision-making process. One word of warning, however, when it comes to the final decisions:

You are the expert when it comes to coaching. Take your players' input if you ask for it, but make final decisions based on your own judgment and expertise.

The *friendly coach* is one who places a priority on relationships with individuals. We may spend more time with and have more influence on our younger players than anyone else but their parents. The friendly coach remembers this and treats all players as individuals. Unfortunately, being a friendly coach is sometimes ineffective because the line of authority is blurred. A friendly coach works well when the players need to feel that they have someone whom they can turn to for understanding and support. But a coach is a person who makes others do things that they don't want to do in order for them to improve. For a player to learn or to increase in her skill level, she must be pushed to perform outside of her comfort zone. Mistakes are made, and many players have a difficult time pushing themselves. The coach's job is to motivate the players to work harder. This is sometimes difficult if you think of the players too much as friends.

Being on a team also requires discipline. The friendly coach might at times find it difficult to push players because of a fear that their relationship could be affected, when in reality the players need to be pushed.

What Style of Coach Are You?

It is worth spending some time examining yourself to determine what coaching style you employ. You are working with young players, and whichever style or blend of styles that you use should be appropriate not only for yourself but also for the girls. Different players respond in different ways to different styles. One style might be appropriate at one time, while another style might work at other times. If you are introducing a new skill and you want your players to focus on performing a difficult activity, an authoritarian style might be best. If you want to give your players an opportunity to decide what skill they would like to work on or what game they would like to play, the CEO approach might work well.

No matter which style you use, it is critical to remember the following: The coach is the leader of the team, and the players need that leadership in order to improve. No matter how the players respond on the outside, your leadership is important for them internally because they are looking to you for answers. Never let the players think that you are unsure of what you are doing, for they could lose confidence in you as their coach.

The Win-at-All-Costs versus Player-Development Philosophy

As with coaching styles, you could also adopt many different coaching philosophies. There are two extremes on a continuum of philosophies, and each coach can find where he or she lies as on the continuum. A coach can employ a player-development philosophy in which the emphasis is placed upon player improvement. Or they might choose to adopt a win-at-all-cost philosophy, in which a premium is placed on victories. Most coaches find their philosophy to be somewhere between the two extremes. The healthiest philosophy for your girls, however, is one that is strongly biased toward player development.

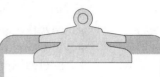

Coaching Tip

A good motivational tool is to allow your players to choose an activity that they can do toward the end of practice if they worked hard at a skill or technique earlier in the day.

There are other issues, such as the level at which you are coaching, that can also have an affect on your philosophy. As with style, your coaching philosophy may also change with experience and with influence from others around you.

What Is a Player-Development Philosophy?

A player-development philosophy is a coaching belief that success is measured by how well your players learn and develop the skills of soccer. Winning is important for the sake of achieving a goal, but it is not your main priority. As a player development-oriented coach, your approach to teaching emphasizes learning and mastering skills. Although it is your duty to show your players how to be successful, and thus to either score goals or stop the other team from scoring, you place a greater emphasis on the players' improvement as individuals. A player-development philosophy does not mean that winning is not important. It is just not the primary measure of success.

An important principle to keep in mind while developing your coaching philosophy is that although soccer is a very simple game, it is also a very complex game. Its simplicity lies with the fact that the game has very few rules and can be played by almost anyone. It is complex because there are many difficult skills and tactics that players need to master to increase their satisfaction and enjoyment in the game. It is impossible to expect players to master difficult concepts without first mastering the fundamentals. This would be the same as trying to teach someone algebra before they mastered addition and subtraction. Unfortunately, many coaches are over-eager, and, for many different reasons, they prefer to teach advanced concepts to beginners, which leads to frustration for both the girls and the coach.

There is a difference between challenging the girls and overwhelming the girls—experience, knowledge, and common sense can help you determine what is appropriate. In general, you will always be safe working on the basics rather than advanced concepts, even with advanced players. You can easily challenge any level player to improve by decreasing the amount of time or space they have to perform the action. The best players in the world are the players who have mastered the fundamentals and can perform them quickly and in tight spaces.

What Is a Win-at-All-Costs Philosophy?

A win-at-all-costs philosophy places winning as the primary measure of success. Player improvement is not as important as winning soccer games. By win-at-all-costs, I am not implying that coaches are willing to break rules and do whatever it takes to win. Instead, a coach with a win-at-all-costs philosophy may emphasize things that will help the team win today, but not necessarily in the future. For example, it is very common for younger players (under 10) to play on a full-sized field. A team might have a very quick player who can run faster than most of her opponents. To win games, the coach may adapt a style of play in which the players are encouraged to hit the ball long and just let the fast player run past everyone to score. The problem is that eventually that quick player is going to have to play against players who are just as swift as she is. If she has not developed the necessary skills to control a ball and to dribble it past a defender, the goal scorer at age 9 might become the average player or the dropout at age 14. This coach is sacrificing future development for present victories.

A common issue that pervades sports today is the increased emphasis on winning. Pressure from parents and spectators can sometimes become overwhelming. In the professional, college, and even the high school and club levels, coaching jobs hinge on a win-loss record. It is common at the end of professional and college sports seasons to see administrators replace coaches because of the high emphasis on results. There is no doubt that winning is important, but the unfortunate thing is that the professional attitude has started to become an issue with youth sports.

Why a Player-Development Philosophy Is Better!

When you practice a player-development philosophy, you will find that there is great satisfaction in helping players improve without regard for week-to-week game results. There are many reasons why coaches are better to adopt a player-development philosophy.

- Increased player satisfaction
- Increased player motivation
- Increased chances for future success
- Increase proficiency in the game

Because soccer is a complex game, players need to learn and master skills and concepts first, in a simple manner. As they become proficient at the basic skills, more complex ideas can be introduced, and the chances of success improve because of a sound foundation.

Developing Your Own Coaching Philosophy

To develop your own coaching philosophy, you need to ask yourself why you are coaching. What is the motivating factor behind your decision to become a coach? Perhaps you had no choice in the matter, because you are a drafted coach or a coach who was forced to take your "volunteer" position. Nevertheless, you need to ask yourself what you are trying to accomplish within your position. Take a minute to reflect upon these questions:

A PLAYER-DEVELOPMENT PHILOSOPHY

One of the teams that I work with is currently the defending state champion and one of the better under-16 girls' squads in the western United States. I began to help coach this team at the request of the group's head coach when the girls were 11 years old. The team had been together for a few years and posted average results in league and tournament play. During once-a-week training sessions, I focused on individual ball mastery. Every week, we worked toward improving ball control, dribbling moves, and touch on the ball. As the players have gotten older, our training focus has changed, and the players are capable of performing the more complex actions because they mastered the basics through repetition. The team went from an average team at 11 to a premier team at 15 years of age. There is no doubt that the team could not be where they are today without the individual training they received when they were younger. Also, when college recruiters come looking, they will not be concerned with the team's level at 11, but rather, their level today.

- Why are you coaching youth?
- What do you define as a successful season?
- How important are winning and losing?
- What are your goals for the season?
- How would you like others to describe you as a coach?
- Does your league or club have a stated philosophy? If so, do you agree or disagree with its mission?

When you have answered these questions, you will become more aware of your coaching philosophy. When answering these questions and developing your coaching philosophy, it is important to take into account that you are coaching young players. Regardless of the skill level and experience of the players, they are still children and must be treated accordingly.

Another tool that you could use to determine your coaching beliefs is a simple quiz from the book *Successful Coaching* by Rainer Martens that assesses your objectives. For each question, place a 3 by the answer that you feel to be most important and a 1 by the answer that you feel to be least important. Put a 2 by the remaining answer.

1. The best coaches are those who

_____ A. Give individuals help and are interested in young athletes' development

_____ B. Make practices and games fun

_____ C. Teach athletes the skills needed to win

2. If a news story were written about me, I would like to be described as

_____ A. A coach who contributed to the development of young people

_____ B. A coach for whom the athletes enjoyed playing

_____ C. A winning coach

3. As a coach I emphasize

_____ A. Teaching skills that young people can use later in life

_____ B. Having fun

_____ C. Winning

Total your score for each letter answer.

_____ A _____ B _____ C

If your highest score was for *A* answers, your priority swings toward the development of young athletes. If *B* answers were your highest score, your priority is toward having fun. If *C* was your highest score, your emphasis is more on winning.

OTHER RESPONSIBILITIES AND ITEMS TO CONSIDER

There are other additional responsibilities that you will have while coaching, including time commitment, legal issues, team discipline, and injury care and prevention.

Time Commitment

Coaching a team requires a time commitment. You are probably a coach or are interested in coaching, but coaching is not your main profession. You may have a full-time job, or you might be a student. You coach to satisfy a personal desire to work with young people. This is a great reason to coach, but the time commitment involved should not be overlooked. Plan on at least two practices a week, a game on the weekend, and some planning time throughout the week.

Training sessions should last as long as your league games. For example, if your team's game length is two 25-minute halves, the total time for the game is about 75 minutes (15-minute warm-up, 50 minutes of actual play, and a 10-minute halftime). It is rare that you will need to go longer than that. Plan on two evenings a week for about 2 hours (travel to and from the practice and setup time), a couple of hours on the weekend, and an occasional meeting or party with the team and parents. There may also be league and club meetings that you need to attend. Find out prior to making a commitment, because you do not want to let the girls down!

Legal and Liability Issues

In today's society, it is common to read or hear about lawsuits filed because of professional negligence. As a coach who is working with young people, you assume responsibility for the minors that you are supervising. If you are not careful, dangerous situations could arise in which you would be held liable. It is important, therefore, that you practice risk management as you coach. Keep the following issues in mind to help reduce the chance of legal problems.

• Provide proper instruction for the skill or exercise. As a coach, you are considered an expert at teaching the required skills of the game. If you provide improper instruction or set up an activity that adversely exposes a player to injury, you could be held liable for injuries.

• Teach skills that are appropriate to the age and skill level of the participants. It is not appropriate to teach a 7-year-old how to head a ball that is coming out of the air from a 16-year-old goalkeeper's punt. Do not have your players perform skills that are too complex and that increase chances of injury.

• Supervise all players at all times. If you turn your back during a practice, or if you leave the area and an injury occurs, you could be held liable. If the players are spread out across the field, or if you do have to leave the area, appoint an assistant or a parent to take over supervision.

• Ensure that the playing or practice areas are safe. Scan all playing areas for items that could cause injuries, such as broken glass, holes, and such.

• Select players who are reasonably appropriate for the team. It is inappropriate to have players competing against each other who are too big or too small as compared with the rest of the group. For instance, it is not appropriate for a highly developed 11-year-old to be playing with 8-year-olds if the 11-year-old could cause an injury to the others as a result of her size. The same goes for players who are too small. Use common sense to avoid problems.

• Make sure that appropriate persons have picked up all players after practices and games. You are responsible for the players' safety until they leave the area with a parent or appropriate escort. Sometimes situations arise where a parent is late picking up a player. It is very important that you and an assistant or another parent wait with the player, because if something were to happen to her, you could be held responsible. Having two people wait will ensure that if something should happen, there is help and a witness nearby. The same issue could also occur before practice. If a parent drops her daughter off before practice and the player injures herself, you could be held responsible even if you have not yet arrived. When meeting with parents, talk about the importance of them being

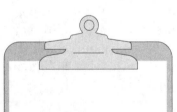

Coaching Tip

Place bags, extra balls, or anything else that a player might trip or fall over away from the field of play.

COACH'S LIABILITY INSURANCE

Because of liability and legal issues, all coaches working with young people should be covered by liability insurance. If you coach at an elementary school or high school, the institution might have coverage. Check with your administrators. Insurance might also be available through your club or league. Many leagues have registration fees that include insurance for all participants. If your league or club does not provide coverage, it is important that you take care of this yourself. Professional organizations, such as the National Soccer Coaches Association of America and the U.S. Soccer Coaches Organization, provide liability insurance as a membership benefit. The cost to join these organizations is very modest (less than $100 a year), and members receive additional advantages. Contact those organizations for information on becoming a member. Also consider purchasing extra insurance if you are planning on running a clinic or camp for a large number of players.

prompt when picking up their daughters. Clearly state what time you will be arriving for each practice so the parents are informed as to when it is appropriate to drop off their daughters.

Team Discipline

As the coach, you must deal with issues concerning individual and team discipline. Learning responsibility and discipline is a great benefit to those who participate in sports. By establishing rules and guidelines of appropriate behavior, for both the girls and their parents, you are creating an environment that is enjoyable to participate in. It is up to you what your rules will be, how many rules you will have, and how you will address in appropriate behavior. Some typical rules might include:

- All players must arrive at all practices and games on time, unless prior arrangements were made with the coaching staff.
- All players must bring a ball, shin guards, and water bottle to each practice and game.
- All players and parents should treat opponents, officials, and team members with dignity and respect.
- All players must pay attention when the coach is speaking.

These are but a few possible rules. It is very important, as difficult as it sometimes may be, to enforce all penalties that result from a player breaking a rule. Failure to do so could cause your team to lose confidence in you or to lose respect for the rules.

Injury Prevention and Treatment

Soccer is an activity in which injuries can and do occur. Injuries, ranging from cuts and scrapes to broken bones, are common. In general, however, with younger players, fewer serious injuries tend to occur. Common injuries include bruises, strains, sprains, and cuts and scrapes. You should have a basic knowledge of how to address these issues. Do not, however, overstep your bounds. Never prescribe a treatment for any injury in which you are unsure. Perhaps you might be lucky enough to have a parent on your team who is a medical professional. If so, solicit his or her help in these matters.

What to Do in Case of Injury

If an injury does occur during practice or a game, the following steps are a good common-sense approach to treating the injury.

1. Identify how the injury occurred. Ask the player, or others who might have witnessed the injury.
2. Ask the player where she is hurt.
3. Make sure the injury is not life threatening. Any injury involving the head or neck should be treated with extreme caution. If the injury is serious, call emergency personnel immediately.
4. Check for swelling or deformities.
5. Compare the injured body part with the opposite body part. For example, with a wrist injury, compare with the other wrist to see if you notice any differences. If you notice any deformities, you may be dealing with a broken bone. The only expert on determining if a bone is broken is a doctor— advise that your player be taken to the hospital or emergency room for further evaluation.

Treating Swelling with the RICE Method

Most injuries that involve swelling or bruising are a result of some collision. A player may get kicked, knocked down, trip, or get hit with the ball. Swelling and bruising occur when blood vessels are broken, resulting in increased blood flow to or decreased fluid removal from the affected areas. In any injury that involves swelling, treat using the RICE principle:

- **Rest.** Remove the player from the game and have her rest the affected body part.
- **Ice.** Apply ice to the injury to reduce swelling. Do not apply ice directly to the skin. Use an ice bag or wrap the ice in a moist cloth and apply that to the affected area. Ice should be applied for no longer than 20 minutes at a time, with at least 20 minutes between icing.
- **Compression.** Wrap the injury with an ace bandage to help reduce blood flow to the area.
- **Elevate.** Elevate the affected area. Place the body part higher than the heart. Gravity will help to reduce fluid flow to the area.

If you use common sense, you will be able to deal with most injuries that occur. However, it is not a bad idea to get certified in first aid and CPR. Most communities offer these courses throughout the year, and spending a weekend afternoon or evening could pay big dividends.

CLINICS AND CERTIFICATION COURSES

In addition to the wealth of information available in this book, new coaches can gain valuable advice and tips by attending coaching clinics and certification courses. Some leagues and clubs require certain levels of certification before a coach is allowed to run a team. If you have never attended a coaching clinic, I would highly recommend doing so. Legendary college basketball coach John Wooden said it best: "It's what you learn after you know it all that counts." Unfortunately many coaches do not attend clinics because they feel that they are already comfortable with the basics of soccer, or that they cannot afford the time or expense to attend. If you are one of those coaches, I hope you will reconsider your position.

There are also several national organizations that offer coaching certification courses. These organizations

Coaching Tip

Items for first-aid kit:
- Bandages of various sizes
- 1–2 ace bandages
- Gauze
- Rubber gloves (always wear when blood is involved)
- Plastic bags (for ice)
- Sun block
- Athletic tape
- Prewrap for taping joints

OVERENTHUSIASTIC COACHES

Coaches often make the assumption that a higher certification is better than a lower or entry-level certification. Because soccer is a complex game, this is not necessarily true. Success in understanding or passing at one level is often highly dependent upon success at a prior level. In addition, much of the material in advanced courses is not applicable to younger players. It is excellent for you to have a goal of increased knowledge, but make sure that you are proficient at your current level before you attempt the next.

offer courses for different levels of coaches, and follow specific certification curriculums.

There are several soccer coaching organizations that provide training opportunities for coaches. United States Soccer (U.S. Soccer), the National Soccer Coaches Association of America (NSCAA), and the American Youth Soccer Organization (AYSO) are all national entities that hold coaching clinics of various levels (see table 1.1). Each organization approaches coaching education in a slightly different manner, which allows individuals to choose the types of clinics they would like to attend. Each organization sponsors clinics that are specific to the level of the coach and to the level of the players being coached. Check with your local state organizations and the Web sites of these groups to find more detailed information.

Table 1.1   Coaching clinics offered by various national entities

	U.S. Soccer	NSCAA	AYSO
A License	National Youth License	National Youth Diploma	National Coaching Course
B License	Youth Module 1, 2, 3	Advanced Regional Diploma	Advanced Coaching Course
C License		Regional Diploma	Intermediate Coaching Course
D License		State Diploma	Youth Coaching Course
E License			U10 Coaching Course
			U8 Coaching Course
			U6 Coaching Course

NSCAA CONVENTION

Each January, the National Soccer Coaches Association of America holds its annual convention. The location of the convention changes from year to year. The convention offers opportunities for coaches of all levels to attend clinics and professional meetings and to meet with fellow coaches. Although the organization is open to membership by coaches of any level, the association has recognized that needs and interests differ depending on coaching experience. The convention, which runs from Thursday through Sunday, has been organized to address these different needs. For coaches who do not have the time or finances to attend a weeklong coaching course, or for those who are looking for additional resources, the convention offers chances to fill those needs.

SUMMARY

Coaching a team requires that you know more than just how to play and teach the game. Having a vast technical knowledge of how soccer is played is helpful, but it is only a small part of what coaching requires. It is just as important to be organized, to know how to communicate, and to be able to work with others. More important, you must remember that you are a role model, and like it or not, your actions will have a lasting affect upon your players and their parents.

When coaching, you need to be aware of your style and your philosophy. A player-development philosophy that places individual improvement ahead of victories is the best and healthiest approach.

Finally, no matter how much coaching experience you have, you can always learn more. Coaching clinics and certification courses are great places not only to learn from expert coaches but also to interact and gain insight from fellow attendees. Like mastering anything else, learning to become a better coach is an ongoing process. Take advantage of the experience of others—as you are doing by reading this book!

2

COACHING STRATEGIES

You are probably reading this book because you are looking for tips and advice on coaching girls' soccer. You may be wondering about the differences between boys and girls, and how you might take these differences into account while working with female athletes.

Much of the current debate about the differences between boys and girls is based on the sociological concerns that define gender roles. Many books, articles, and position papers addressing this issue have been published. Scientific literature concerning the differences, however, is not as deep. Many of the ideas expressed in the literature about the gender differences noticed when coaching girls are based on personal experience and opinion.

A prevalent theory explaining the differences between boys and girls is that long-established gender stereotypes are responsible for the differences between the genders. Traditionally, boys have received sports equipment as gifts, while girls have received dolls and home-making toys. From the time they are born, children are influenced by specific roles and expectations. This, however, is changing, as sports participation by girls is more prevalent than ever: Participation by girls and women in athletics has grown immensely over the past decade and is at an all-time high.

As a male coach who has worked extensively with females, I can say that there genuinely are gender differences that must be taken into account when coaching girls and boys. However, these differences are mainly concerned with communication and motivation. Boys and girls can and should be coached similarly. Soccer can be played by almost everyone, with equal chances for success. There is a place for big and short, fast and slow. This is one reason that the sport is so popular and attractive. The rules are the same no matter who is playing, as are the techniques, tactics, physical demands, and psychological requirements. There may be different approaches in tactics and styles of play as players grow older because there are physiological differences between the sexes. However, while the players are young, you can be a very successful coach applying the same principles to boys and girls.

Many of the concepts addressed throughout this chapter apply equally toward coaching girls or boys. In sections that discuss specific approaches for girls, I am not stating that boys and girls are necessarily different, but rather that the concepts discussed have been found to be effective with girls.

EFFECTIVE COMMUNICATION SKILLS

To be a successful coach, you need to be an effective communicator. Think back to your favorite coaches or teachers. Chances are that they were very effective communicators. This skill may have may have seemed very natural for some of your coaches, but they all had to work to achieve their communication skills.

While you are coaching, you will have to interact with many individuals and groups. Some of those groups, such as referees, league officials, and opposing coaches, are people whom you will work with only occasionally. There are two groups, however, that you will interact with frequently and with whom you must establish effective communications: your players and their parents.

There are going to be times when you come to practice or a game with something else on your mind. Perhaps something has happened at work, or maybe you are dealing with a personal issue. No matter what the cause, it has nothing to do with your players. If you let this outside issue change the way you act toward your team, the girls will sense that there is a problem. There is a great chance that they will think they have done something wrong or have made you unhappy. As you well know, they are not the primary reason for your unhappiness. It is vital that you make every effort to treat the girls as they should be treated at all times, and not differently depending upon your mood. The best thing to help you get through difficult times off the field may be to recognize the positive efforts of the girls. This approach not only lets the girls know that you are behind them, but it may also help to make you feel better!

Communicating with Players

You will communicate with your players more than any other group. Your ability to teach, explain, instruct, and motivate is very critical. The methods you use to communicate with your athletes can vary, and your team will interpret more than just what you say when you interact with them. The actual words that you use are but a small part of the interaction that occurs when communicating: Language is important, but so are voice tone, eye contact, and body language. Many times your words are not heard because the other signals that you are projecting have distracted the players or have obstructed what you are actually saying.

Verbal Communication

When speaking to your team, whether with an individual, a small group, or the entire squad, speak so that you are easy to hear and use words that are easy to understand. Avoid jargon or soccer terminology that the players may find difficult to grasp. In addition, you should never use or permit your players to use profanity. The tone of your voice is also important. Speak in an enthusiastic manner and encourage your players to pay attention and focus on the task at hand.

When instructing an individual, look directly at her when you speak. Your players, no matter what age, must understand that you respect them and their thoughts. Looking at your players when you speak to them will help build their self-confidence and self-esteem. Players will feel important because they have your undivided attention. Similarly, when speaking with groups, make sure that you have everyone's attention and that you can make eye contact with everyone with whom you are speaking. You might have to draw the players closer to you, to be sure that everyone can hear. Stand in a place where you can face the entire team. If it is a windy day, face the team so you are speaking with the wind. If it is a sunny day, stand so you are facing the sun. If there are other activities or potential distractions nearby, try to stand so that your team is facing away from the distractions.

Nonverbal Communication

Players pick up on your body actions when you are speaking to them. Sometimes unwanted messages are transmitted. Other times you can use your body language purposely to emphasize a point. Simple things like smiling or frowning can affect how your message is interpreted. Consider the following situation: Your team has been working on passing the ball with the instep. One of your players, Katie, attempts a pass but inadvertently uses her toe. You make the comment, "C'mon Katie, try to hit the ball with your shoelaces." A pretty innocent coaching point, but if it is accompanied by a smile, it will be received much more effectively than if it were delivered with a frown or a stern look.

If you feel that you need work with your nonverbal communication, or if you are unsure whether you are projecting conflicting messages with your body language, consider asking an assistant coach for feedback. Do this away from the field or after the players have all departed, but be open to any advice. This takes courage, but it is extremely helpful. Asking for feedback might help you recognize things that you might not have been aware of before.

Written Communication

You may need to write letters to your players or provide handouts about strategies or concepts. When working with older players, this is a great method to help them master difficult ideas or tactics. For younger girls, a simple note prior to or after the season can mean a lot. Use common sense when putting things down on paper, and make sure that all communication is appropriate.

Communicating with Parents

Positive relationships with your players' parents are very important. Parents can be either your biggest supporters or your worst enemies. You hope that you will be blessed with parents who support you and your objectives. Unfortunately, you may have parents who judge your coaching ability by how much playing time their child receives.

Treat your team's parents as if they were your players. Communicate with them about your concerns and your intentions for the season and any specific situations. Often you will find that by keeping the parents apprised of information and involved, they will be much easier to work with. Use a preseason team meeting (discussed in chapter 10), to create a positive, informative relationship from the beginning. Unfortunately, despite your best efforts, you will encounter problems with some of your players' parents. Chapter 3 provides some strategies and advice for dealing with these situations.

Improving Your Communication Skills

There are many ways to improve your communication skills. Many successful coaches, political figures, and business leaders have published books about how to achieve success. Almost all of these people were effective communicators and their books are full of good advice.

You may also consider attending seminars and workshops designed to help improve communication skills. Check your local newspaper or continuing education institution to find potential classes. Groups like Dale Carnegie offer courses specifically designed to help individuals improve their human relations skills.

But reading and attending classes or seminars are not enough. You also must make a personal effort to practice. Effective communication is a skill—just like kicking a soccer ball—and the only way that improvement and change can occur is through continued practice. You might have to leave your comfort zone, but once you do so, growth occurs.

EFFECTIVE TEACHING

One of your primary duties as a coach is to teach. Not only will you teach the obvious topics like techniques and tactics, but you'll also have the opportunity to reinforce discipline, respect for others, cooperation, and time management. Many of your players are involved in multiple activities. Sometimes, especially if the girl or her parents are not experienced at identifying the time commitments required for various activities, the child can become overscheduled. Therefore, you may find yourself having to introduce time management concepts to your players. Be sure to impress on them that commitments are important and should be honored. Whatever you are teaching, your method and instruction need to be sound, correct, and clearly understood. Your players will learn more quickly and be more attentive when practices are fun and appropriate.

Because mistakes can and do occur, one of the most important attributes you must have is patience. Without patience, teaching becomes ineffective. It is even possible that your players can regress in their abilities.

If you ask your players why they play soccer, you will get many answers. One probable answer is to please others, including their parents and their coaches. The next time you are at practice, try the following exercise: Have all players juggle, and say to the entire team, "Who can juggle the ball ten times before it hits the ground?" If ten is too easy or too hard, select an appropriate number that is difficult but achievable. Watch how your team reacts. You will have many players working on the task, while frequently looking to see if you are watching. If they are successful at meeting the challenge, they will surely call out or run over to you to make sure you know they were successful. They want to please you! A good coach realizes this and uses it to help enhance learning by recognizing players' successes at every opportunity.

There are two approaches you can take toward anything in life—positive and negative. A positive approach implies an upbeat, enthusiastic outlook, while a negative approach usually means depression and disappointment. You can be a positive or a negative coach by what you choose to focus on and how you make corrections. Keep in mind that players react better to positive coaching. You can coach positively by making a point of reinforcing successful performance. If you are working on a technique, recognize what the athlete did correctly, even if it is only a portion of the entire movement. Motor skills are acquired through successful repetition, and experts in the field of motor learning have shown that feedback enhances the learning process. When you point out correct aspects of performance, not only do you help to increase the girls' confidence, but you also help them understand what the correct action looks and feels like.

Please do not think that a positive coach can never get mad nor show disapproval. Remember that players want to please, and showing disapproval can be a powerful motivator toward changing actions. A positive coach will not get upset if a skill is performed incorrectly if effort was made and the mistake was honest. By recognizing effort, your coaching will become positive, and you will find that the girls will respond.

There will be times when you have to point out mistakes. A common issue faced when coaching is dealing with players who feel that pointing out their mistakes is personal. They have a hard time understanding that the feedback is meant to make them better. The trick is to determine when to point out mistakes and how often to make coaching points without affecting the player's motivation. An additional issue when dealing with feedback is that players are individuals. Each player will react in a different way. Therefore, using the sandwich approach to applying criticism is a great way to make all players realize that you do not feel that they do everything wrong.

Coaches who use the sandwich approach to giving criticism take the negative, or corrective, statement and "sandwich" it between two positive statements. The positive statements identify something the player is doing that is correct, while the negative statement identifies the mistake and how it can be corrected. Consider the following example: During a shooting exercise, Lori continues to shoot the ball over the goal. You have analyzed her shot and see that the cause of her problem is that she keeps leaning back when striking the ball, causing the ball to fly upward. As a player, which comment would you respond to better?

Lori, quit hitting the ball over the goal! Place it on net!

or

Lori, you are doing a great job of approaching the ball, but when you are striking the ball, you are leaning back. This is causing the ball to fly upward over the goal. Try to keep your head down and stay over the ball when following through, and the ball will stay lower.

The first comment does not tell the player anything that she does not already know, and probably adds to her frustration. The second statement utilizes the sandwich technique. Its effectiveness is obvious. It provides a concrete solution to the problem, and it also provides encouragement. Use the sandwich approach and coach positively so that your teaching is more effective.

Make Challenges and Training Fun

Girls play soccer because it is fun. To build on that fun, try to make your practice sessions as fun as possible *and* create an environment in which learning occurs. Set up practice games that use soccer skills but that also involve competition. The contest could be player against player, group against group, or even a person against herself. For instance, to pit a player against herself, encourage each player to juggle a ball and establish a personal record of how many times she can keep the ball in the air before it hits the ground; then have players try to improve their own records. If you recognize the player who gets the highest score, you place individual against individual. If you have players juggle in groups of two or more, then you not only allow groups to compete against one another, but you also help improve cooperation and teamwork.

Your challenge is to create and implement activities that are fun. Ask fellow coaches for advice. Consider using games that do not involve soccer, but add a ball to them. Freeze tag is a fun game that is played by children at school; if each player dribbles a ball while she plays, you now have a game that is fun *and* improves soccer skills.

Make Challenges and Training Appropriate

It is important that your practice activities are not only fun, but that they are also appropriate for the age and skill level of the members of your team. Keep this in mind in both directions—some activities can

HOW TO HANDLE A WIDE VARIETY OF SKILL LEVELS

In a perfect world, all of your players would be at the same skill level, and it would be easy to design and use appropriate training games and exercises. In reality, this is improbable and untrue. Here are some suggestions for dealing with this dilemma:

- **Do away with elimination games.** Elimination games are activities in which players who fail leave the game. For example, in the dribbling game called Knockout, each player has a ball and attempts to kick the other players' balls out of the playing area while keeping control of her own. If a player's ball is knocked out, that player is eliminated from the game. The last person left in the area is the winner. The problem is that the people who need the most work on keeping the ball are probably the ones who are eliminated first because of their skill deficit. Instead, consider changing Knockout to a teaching game. When a ball is hit out of the area, rather than eliminating the player, have her perform a simple penalty (ball touches, pushups) before rejoining the game. This keeps everyone active and provides all players with more learning opportunities.

- **Adjust challenges among individuals.** If some of your players can perform a skill correctly while others are struggling, increase the challenge for those who have mastered the skill or have them work on mastering a subtle aspect of the technique. For instance, if you are working on a dribbling fake, those who have the footwork down can work on executing the move faster or on perfecting the upper body movement associated with the fake.

- **Adjust the criteria for success among individuals.** When breaking your team into small groups, manipulate pairings so the less skilled players are paired together and the more skilled players are partners. During training, give those who are having problems a greater amount of feedback. Do not ignore those who are doing well, but spend more time coaching those who are having problems. Everyone can be working at the same time; you are just adjusting how you apply feedback.

be too easy while others can be too hard. A good rule of thumb is to analyze the activity or exercise during the first few minutes that the players are working. Is this task too easy? Is it too difficult? Are the players experiencing enough success to keep them interested but not so much that they are bored? Answering these questions can help you determine if the activity is appropriate.

Have Patience!

Mastering anything takes time and patience. The ability to remain positive despite the mistakes that will occur is critical for you as a coach working with young athletes. Your players are children, not little adults, and they will make mistakes. Although it can and will be frustrating, especially when mistakes are repeated, it is important that you maintain your composure and remind yourself that the girls are trying. Remember that the girls want to please you.

Females are very relationship oriented. Although this may not be as apparent with younger girls, it certainly should be kept in mind when coaching any team. If you lose your patience when your players are trying their best, you might make your players feel that you are unhappy with them as people. As trying as it can sometimes be, it is important that the players feel that you believe in them. This helps increase their motivation to improve.

EFFECTIVE TEAM DISCIPLINE

Team discipline involves maintaining order among your team. Effective teams and coaches have a defined form of team discipline. Some coaches prefer to have a multitude of rules; others would rather have as few rules as possible. Some coaches like to put their rules in writing, while others communicate their wishes at team meetings or directly to the players and their parents. (Rules must be explained to the parents, partly because any rules regarding punctuality will usually depend upon the parents ensuring proper arrival time.) Regardless of how many rules you decide upon and how you choose to express them, it is important that you give some thought to this issue.

All teams and groups require guidelines for appropriate and inappropriate behavior. As a youth coach, it is up to you to determine what rules you wish to have your players and parents follow. Keep your rules as simple as possible. In addition, keep the following in mind when deciding upon your team's rules:

PUNISH THE PLAYER OR THE PARENT?

One of the most frustrating things you may have to deal with is a player who arrives late to practices and games. You want players to show up on time, but you are facing a dilemma: If your girls rely upon their parents to get them to practice on time, is it their fault or their parents' fault that the child is tardy?

Here is an effective approach to this dilemma. If the child is late once or twice, a comment to the entire group at the end of practice, when the parents can hear, about the importance of being on time may solve the problem. If lateness is repeated, speak directly to the parents about the importance of getting their daughter to practice on time. Suggest alternative transportation, like carpooling, if it's appropriate. Above all, be very flexible. Chances are that soccer is not the parents' greatest priority, especially if they have other children.

You can also design practices so you start with individual skill work that focuses on a technique that has been introduced at an earlier practice. Each player should have a ball and should be working on some technical skill or playing a game involving individuals or partners. If players are late, rather than disrupting practice, they can easily begin playing when they arrive. Start teaching new skills once everyone is present.

1. Select rules with a reason. If a parent or player questions a rule, you need to be able to explain why you have decided upon it. If you cannot provide a good, logical answer, it probably is not a good rule.
2. Establish what the consequence will be if a rule is broken. Different rules will warrant different consequences, so act accordingly.

Players Want Structure

As much as players may test the rules, they want structure. It is this structure that lets them know what is appropriate. When you explain or describe an activity to your team, they will want to know what they can and cannot do. Enforce the rules of all games and activities. This is a big part of their play.

Preach Respect Among Teammates

Respect for others is an important concept that you should address when you are explaining your team's rules. Sports teach people about cooperation and teamwork. These concepts require that teammates respect and work with one another. This is referred to as *team chemistry*. Teams who have good team chemistry get along with each other and work efficiently as a group. Teams without good team chemistry may have the best players, but often the team fails because of a lack of cooperation among members.

Aggressiveness can be defined as a person acting toward another in a hostile or overly detrimental way. Researchers have found that aggressiveness is apparent in children, but more important, males tend to be more physically aggressive, and females tend to be more relationally aggressive. Boys tend to get in physical fights and will push the rules of games as far as possible. Girls, on the other hand, tend not to get in physical fights, but rather, they carry out their aggression through their interactions. Forming cliques, excluding others from groups, and gossiping are typical expressions of relational aggression. You need to monitor and address this at all times. Team chemistry and relational aggression issues become more prevalent as players get older, but it is something that you should always be aware of as you coach a girl's team.

EFFECTIVE MOTIVATION

Motivating people involves getting them to perform and complete some action. Sometimes motivation is very easy; sometimes it is very difficult. Sometimes your job involves encouraging players to work on skills. Other times, you'll need to get them to work hard at a specific exercise or activity. As a motivator, you are actually a salesperson. It is your job to convince the players that what you want them to do is good for them and will help them become better athletes.

We have all heard of coaches who have gained reputations as "master motivators." Each of these persons has been successful at getting individuals to perform at their highest potential. Most coaches have to learn through experience what will work and what will not. Encouragement, positive coaching, and reinforcement of success usually prove to be effective forms of motivation. Understanding the reasons why your players are participating can also help you to determine ways to motivate.

There are many reasons that children choose to participate in sports: They want to have fun, their friends or siblings play, they find satisfaction in accomplishment, or their parents want them to participate. According to Bobby Howe, former Director of Coaching Education for U.S. Soccer, "Surveys of young players over the last few years have shown that the primary reason for players under 12 dropping out of soccer is that they were not having fun."

Having fun is an obvious priority for all the players on your team. If the players are not having fun, they will probably not stay with your team or with the sport. Make the atmosphere at games and practices fun, and your players will have increased enjoyment. They will work harder to improve. Making practice fun does not mean letting the players do whatever they please, nor does it mean that practices consist only of fun games or scrimmages. Scrimmages are an important part of practice, but if you plan on just scrimmaging during practice, you will probably find that your players lose interest or that fun decreases because learning does not occur as effectively as it would during a structured practice. (More is presented about this topic in chapter 5.)

How do you make a practice fun? "Having fun" can mean different things, but for the sake of this book, let's say that an athlete is having fun when she is mentally occupied with completing a task that brings satisfaction. Have your players perform activities that make them concentrate and that result in satisfaction when completed correctly. Provide opportunities for your players to accomplish goals and you will enhance their enjoyment.

Another reason that girls participate in soccer is that their friends and/or siblings do. Perhaps they were encouraged to join a team because they knew others on the team, or maybe an older brother's or sister's involvement spurred their interest. Either way, the relationship aspect of being on a team is of vital importance to young girls.

One of the relationships that girls will value is their relationship with you. It is important to them that you care about them as people, above and beyond being soccer players. They want to know that you like them regardless of how well they play, and if they do make a mistake they often feel that they let you, the coach, down. It is important to be aware of this from both a positive and negative manner. On the positive side, express satisfaction whenever you witness players try or complete an action successfully. This will help increase players' drive to continue to perform correctly. When they see that you are pleased with their effort, they will try to repeat their actions.

On the negative side, if they make mistakes, it is important that you exhibit patience. React in a manner that lets them know that you recognize that they tried and have confidence that they will be successful the next time. They need to know that you still have confidence in them and in their ability. If you portray dissatisfaction, they may feel that you do not like them any more, which can affect future performance.

People also play sports because of the satisfaction they gain when they do something well. Observe the faces of your players the next time you have them practice a skill and they perform it correctly. The more difficult the skill, the more intense the satisfaction. In soccer, players receive this sort of satisfaction because they are forced to use body parts, like their heads and feet, that they might not be comfortable with. Players often want to share their new skills with their parents. When parents congratulate a player and express their delight, her need for satisfaction is fulfilled.

Keep in mind this need for satisfaction when working with your team. Positive coaching and recognition of the players' individual and group accomplishments during games and practices can be a great source of satisfaction for the players. Your acknowledgment of their efforts is important. Appealing to the players' need for satisfaction will increase their motivation to perform.

In some instances, a player might be on your team because her parents or friends want her to play. Perhaps her parents realize the benefits sports play in helping young girls develop, or maybe they just decided that this was a cheap form of childcare. Regardless of the reason, the player might not want to be there. This will be a great motivational challenge because the player has no intrinsic motivation to play.

It is not your fault that the player does not want to play. However, chances are that a girl in this situation, especially a young girl, will be open to trying something new. The problem is that she also might be intimidated, especially if she has never played before. The best thing that you can do is have her participate in fun games that involve a soccer ball but that are not necessarily soccer related. She might already be experienced with playing games like Tag and Red Light, Green Light. Include a ball, and now she is playing the game while learning the skills of soccer. For U8 (under age eight) players, these games should be a large portion of your practice sessions already!

By taking this approach, the players will become motivated to play and will often have fun without thinking about soccer. They will associate soccer with having fun, and they will be hooked. If you take this approach, and the child still does not want to play, the parents will probably make a change themselves.

INTRINSIC VERSUS EXTRINSIC MOTIVATION

Motivation can be either intrinsic or extrinsic. Intrinsic motivation is motivation from within. A person is internally motivated when she wants to do something because of the satisfaction received. Extrinsic motivation is motivation resulting from outside sources. Extrinsic motivation can be positive, such as when a player receives an award. But it can also be negative, such as when a player makes a decision as a result of fear. A player might not choose to complete an action because she thinks she will get in trouble or be punished.

As a coach, you should strive to help your players become intrinsically motivated. When players are intrinsically motivated, they are more apt to work on skills on their own and find enjoyment through participating. Here are some ways to increase intrinsic motivation:

1. **Set goals.** Help your players set goals, and then monitor their progress toward achieving those goals. Goals can be team- or individual-based and should be difficult, but achievable. (Use individual goals with younger players.) One player's individual goal might be to juggle the ball in the air a certain number of times before it hits the ground.

2. **Recognize effort.** By recognizing effort, you work with a player's desire for satisfaction and desire to please others. Make every effort to let players know when you are pleased with their performance.

3. **Make practices fun.** If training is fun, players look forward to participating. Introduce new activities and work on various skills. Try not to run the same session twice. You can repeat exercises, but make some change—the field size, number of players, or small rule changes. For younger players, renaming an exercise is often enough to make things different.

Treat Your Players as Athletes

When working with players, treat them as athletes. Recognize that they are soccer players. Often giving the girls an expectation to live up to will make them meet your own expectations. Refer to the girls as your players, and point out things that you notice other soccer players doing that reflect what you would like your players to do. This approach will instill pride and a sense of purpose within your team.

SUMMARY

Effective coaching requires much more than technical knowledge of soccer. You need to have a sound coaching philosophy, solid teaching skills, and a thorough understanding of the art of communication. Awareness of your verbal and nonverbal communication methods will help you become a more effective communicator.

Maintaining proper team discipline is also important. Members of any team or group are expected to act appropriately, and one of your jobs is to define proper behavior. In addition to determining what is allowable, you also have to enforce the rules, which involves determining punishments and rewards. You need to be able to motivate your athletes to perform, because there will be times when the girls will have trouble concentrating or will choose to mess around. Exhibit patience and, while creating a fun atmosphere, encourage your players to work toward improvement. Treat your girls as athletes, but keep in mind that they are also children.

3

COACHING GIRLS

COACHES WHO WORK WITH females often wonder about the differences in coaching boys and girls. Perhaps you have questions like these:

- Do I need to treat girls differently than boys?
- Do girls practice and play differently than boys?
- Do girls and boys grow differently?
- Are there any skills or techniques that girls perform differently than boys?
- What kinds of approaches will work better when coaching girls?
- Do I need to be aware of any issues that may come up when coaching girls?
- As a male coaching girls, what special issues should I be aware of?
- Are girls motivated differently than boys?

This chapter will explore these questions and will provide you with ideas and methods to help solve potential problems. One thing to remember, however, is that many of the anecdotes that are detailed in this chapter are simply that—stories that illustrate a point. Many of the ideas presented are backed by hard research, but in general this area is filled with large amounts of hearsay.

Much of the research literature theorizes that differences between boys and girls can be explained by cultural expectations. The stereotypical boy receives sports equipment while the girl receives a dollhouse. When girls decided to play a sport like soccer, differences were attributed to the thought that they were not as successful because they did not have prior experience with exercise and competition. Other explanations about lack of female participation or performance differences between boys and girls were that girls did not want to be considered to be tomboys or that they were afraid of developing big muscles. Cultural expectations result in more differences, and an ongoing circle of cause and effect.

If differences between boys and girls are a result of society and cultural expectations, then it should follow that if the expectations were changed or were similar from the start between boys and girls, the differences between boys and girls would start to disappear. I believe that this is true, and is particularly evident in sport participation. With the passing of Title IX, which requires that equal athletic opportunities be given to girls and boys at educational institutions, the sporting world has undergone huge changes. Participation by girls in soccer has increased dramatically at all levels. In many soccer leagues, there are as many, or even more, girls playing than boys.

There are differences between males and females that you must take into account when coaching girls as opposed to boys, but it is very important that you keep the following statement in mind:

Coach the athlete, not the gender!

Soccer players are soccer players, regardless of whether they are male or female. The techniques, tactics, and fitness demands of soccer are no different for girls than they are for boys. You may have to adjust your approach or coaching style, but this could be the case when coaching boys as well, because individuals respond to different forms of motivation. You may also have to deal with specific issues that occur more often with girls than with boys, especially as the girls enter and complete puberty. However, in general, boys and girls, if coached properly, require similar coaching techniques.

DIFFERENCES IN PLAY

Boys and girls play in relatively similar ways; however, boys usually act more physically aggressive toward each other. Girls, on the other hand, exhibit more relational aggression. (See chapter 2.) While they may be less likely to get into physical fights, they are more likely to form cliques and attempt to leave others out. Most of the differences between boys and girls develop after the age of 10, with the onset of puberty.

There is no evidence that boys and girls perform the techniques and tactics of soccer differently. When coaching girls, you can use many of the same approaches used for coaching boys. While you should not change the types of skills you work on or lower your expectations, you should take care to encourage teamwork and inclusion of all team members. Because girls have been shown to exhibit more psychological aggression toward others than do boys, you may have to deal with more mental conflict than physical conflict. When breaking the team into groups, for example, watch to see if the same players gravitate toward each other, frequently leaving the same teammates out. If this occurs, you need to step in and assign partners or groups. Team chemistry is an important issue that you must always keep an eye on.

PHYSICAL DIFFERENCES

Prior to puberty, there are few physical differences between boys and girls. Differences can be attributed more to individual characteristics and less to gender. Girls tend to reach puberty earlier than boys do: around the ages of 7–14, while boys go through puberty around the ages of 9–16. When these age spans have been reached, physiological changes occur that result in the differences between females and males. Therefore, you will be coaching players who not only are trying to master the skills necessary for soccer, but are also dealing with their rapidly changing bodies.

Size and Strength

Prior to puberty, boys and girls are relatively similar. It is common for teams of players under the age of 10 (U10) to be coed. This is perfectly acceptable. Many times it is more convenient for boys and girls to play together. For instance, children ages eight and younger have a difficult time grasping the fact that they are on a team. They might know that the play on the Bandits, or that they are on Coach John's team, but the concept of cooperation with one another is not understood. Most playing at this stage in the children's lives is self-centered. The gender of teammates is not an issue.

Puberty and Its Onset

For boys and girls, the body undergoes many physical changes with the onset of puberty. There is an increased rate of growth and a change in the level of certain hormones produced by the body: testosterone and estrogen. Females and males both produce each hormone. Testosterone, which causes increased muscle mass, is produced in greater levels in men, whereas estrogen, which results in wider hips and greater body fat, is produced in greater levels in women. Some researchers have also suggested that testosterone production results in increased levels of aggression, which might explain why males tend to be more aggressive than females.

As adolescents complete the puberty process, differences between males and females will become more apparent. During puberty, however, the athletes will be changing at different rates, and it is difficult to point out differences between boys and girls that will be the same for everyone. When coaching players who are experiencing puberty, there are several things to keep in mind:

• **Changing body size.** Proficiency at soccer requires that a person be able to use many body parts and be able to be change directions while controlling the ball. Mastering these skills requires that players learn how to control their bodies. As adolescents undergo changes in the lengths of their legs and arms and changes in body weight, they frequently have to "relearn" some of the skills they could perform prior to puberty. It is not that they forgot how to perform the actions, but rather that they are working with a new body. This relearning may have to occur repeatedly, because puberty may last over the course of a couple of seasons. Therefore, continued and repeated emphasis on technical work should be your greatest teaching priority.

• **Self-consciousness.** With the onset of puberty, not only does the entire body undergo a period of increased growth, but also individual body parts mature. Physically the girls develop into women, with changes in breast size and width of hips. Although this is a normal part of growing, individuals who reach puberty earlier than their friends or later than their peers may become self-conscious about their bodies. It is important to treat all of your players with kindness and respect and to be sympathetic to those who might be embarrassed. If you continue to coach your players as athletes, not as girls, then the self-confidence that they gain from playing soccer can help alleviate their concerns.

• **Discovery of the opposite sex.** As girls go through puberty, they may become interested in boys. Sometimes the interest can become an issue that results in a girl leaving the team. As coach, foster a player-development philosophy and use positive coaching techniques. This may help prevent drop-outs because you are creating an environment in which the girls enjoy participating.

Menstruation

A major change that occurs with the onset of puberty in females is the start of the menstrual cycle. In addition to the emotional changes that accompany the start of the cycle, the young women also experience physical changes that you should be aware of. Symptoms that accompany menstruation include cramping, water retention (bloating), and body aches. This is a very touchy issue, especially if you are a male coaching females. Treat each player with compassion and care. If a player complains that she is not feeling well, encourage her to continue playing. However, let her know that she may sit out if she feels the need to.

If the girls are going to continue to compete as they get older, they will have to learn how to play while going through their periods. I am not advocating that you push the girls when they are not feeling well. Rather, it is appropriate to let them make the decision about playing or sitting on the side. If you are unsure of how to handle this and other situations related to menstruation, speak with the players' parents. They can be extremely helpful during these situations.

Performance Differences

In the past, it was commonly thought that women were not capable of performing at the same level as males. But there is no evidence to support this, and this conclusion is rapidly changing. For instance, when women first started running in organized marathons, there was more than an hour and half difference between the fastest man and the fastest woman. While males have improved the world record time of the marathon as years have passed, so have females, but at a much greater rate.

Females have been approaching the same performance results as that of males in many activities. The difference between males and females that seems to have the largest influence on performance is the fact that, in general, males tend to have a greater amount of muscle mass than females. The greater muscle mass allows for greater amounts of strength and power. This trait, of course, becomes more prevalent after puberty. Although you are working with players who have not yet reached or completed puberty, knowledge of this fact can help you train your players now for future success.

On the soccer field, the strength of male and female players translates into two major differences. First, the fact that males tend to have greater strength allows them to kick balls harder and farther than females can. Most advanced male soccer players can strike a ball across the width of a full-sized soccer field (more than 70 yards). Females have a difficult time accomplishing this because they are just not strong enough. Males can often make up for lack of technique by using more strength.

Second, males tend to play faster than females because of their greater strength and power. Power is the ability to move a certain amount of weight in a certain period of time. Greater power results from moving the same amount of weight in a shorter period of time or a greater amount of weight in the same period of time. However, the fact that males tend to play faster is not necessarily a good thing. Part of mastering a skill is becoming efficient at performing quickly. Many times boys will play soccer faster than they should. Their speed exceeds their ability to execute techniques correctly, and they turn their soccer game into a sloppy affair. The best players are those who realize this and either slow their game down to match their ability or increase their ability to match their speed.

CO-ED TEAMS OR SEPARATE TEAMS?

Should boys and girls play on the same team? This is a frequent question, asked by parents and coaches, who often want to know what is best for a player's development. The answer is that the best team for a girl to play on is the team where she receives the best experience. Sometimes this a co-ed team, sometimes not.

Individuals begin puberty at different times, but a common cutoff age to separate prepubescents from those experiencing puberty is 9–10 years of age. Below this age, co-ed teams work out fine. It is not wrong to separate boys and girls, but it is also not necessary. At the ages of 10 and above, however, teams usually become more gender specific, which is also fine. There are times when an all-boys team will include a girl or two. This may be because there are not enough all-girls teams available or because a girl has been playing on the same team for a number of years. If the girls are not overwhelmed and are learning proper techniques and tactics of the game, a co-ed team does not pose a problem.

Many experienced girls might need to play with boys to get the right level of challenge. The boys might not be as fundamentally good as she is, but because they are faster, they actually help to challenge the gifted athlete. By the age of 14, serious players tend to separate themselves, but co-ed teams do still exist. If the coach and parents are comfortable with a girl receiving the challenge she needs on a boys' team, there should not be any problem.

When coaching young girls, take what is going to happen to their bodies in the future into account. Because they will have difficulty masking a lack of proper technique with strength, it is vital that you work with them to perfect technique. In addition, because they will have difficulty hitting long balls, they need to become proficient at short passes and at accurately placing shots on goal. Do not neglect the practice of shooting balls hard. Just because females, in general, have less muscle mass than males have does not mean that they cannot improve. Work on improving the girls' jumping ability, heading, and leg strength, and perhaps in the future other differences between males and females will also disappear.

PSYCHOLOGICAL DIFFERENCES

As with physical differences between boys and girls, psychological differences do not become apparent until puberty. Prior to that time, boys and girls are very similar, and probably participate in sports for similar reasons. Players play because they want to have fun. They also have the need to belong to a group, the desire to compete, and the compulsion to master the skills involved. As the girls become older, they still express these same reasons for participating. It will become apparent, however, that girls tend to behave in a slightly different manner than boys. When you coach the young girls, you should take this into account.

Why Girls Play

In general, girls tend to be more group oriented than boys are. Part of the reason that girls play is to gain satisfaction from the relationships formed on the team. Play is as important for social growth as it is for physical exercise. While boys may view their teammates as people whom they play soccer with, girls tend to see their teammates as their friends.

Boys' teams can function well even if the players do not get along. Even though the players might not like each other, boys will usually put problems on the back burner when competing. This is not true with girls. Girls tend to hold grudges longer than boys do, as evidenced by their tendency to exhibit more relational aggression. Failure to cooperate will often result in on-field problems.

What Girls Value

Girls are more relationship oriented than boys are. They place a high amount of value in what others think of them and how they fit within the group. Try to pay attention to each player individually as often as possible. Many times a simple greeting will fill their need to be recognized. If you make a big deal about something, such as a great play or even a new pair of shoes, you help them feel empowered. These issues become more prevalent as the girls get older. It is appropriate for you to practice these things now.

What Motivates Girls

A major difference between boys and girls comes in how they are motivated. Most boys play sports to satisfy a personal need to compete. Pleasing others might also be a reason, but probably not as large as personal gratification is. Girls, on the other hand, tend to be motivated more by pleasing others. Use this knowledge to help you motivate your athletes.

Motivate boys by appealing to how they, as individuals, will benefit from their work. Motivate girls by appealing to how their work affects the results of the team. Let them know when you are happy with them. Girls often lose interest in performing because they feel that they could not satisfy their coach, when in fact, the coach was very happy with their performance. It is important that you demonstrate your satisfaction, and not just assume that they know you are happy.

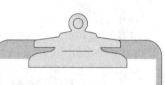

Coaching Tip

When making a coaching point, explaining how an action or lack of action affects the team often appeals to the girls' needs for positive relationships with their teammates and, thus, is very effective.

Girls tend to value relationships more than boys do. It is important when coaching girls that you frequently let them know that even if you are unhappy with their play, it has not affected how you view them as a person. You will have difficulty motivating girls if you say or do anything that affects your relationship with them. Actions like criticizing in public, not speaking with them, and not recognizing their effort can undermine your team.

SERIOUS ISSUES IN SOCCER TODAY

With the increased level of participation by girls in all sports, there has also been an increased level of awareness concerning issues that may affect some of your players. Issues such as eating disorders and sexual harassment are important concerns. You also have to deal with parents and help your girls cope with the stress of competition.

The Female Athlete Triad

As girls grow and become involved in sport and physical activity, they also become susceptible to problems that are directly affected by their nutritional intake. Athletes face different nutritional needs than do non-active people. Those who are training intensely often burn more calories and expend more energy. Unfortunately, it is also common for athletes to leave their diets unaltered. Perhaps they have not been educated about what constitutes a proper diet. Pressures by society to maintain a slender or thin figure often result in the increased desire to maintain a low body weight. "Fad diets" are advertised heavily in an attempt to convince the public that the diet will solve all of the nutritional needs and weight loss issues necessary to maintain perfect health. While many of these diets do have some plausible basis for success, the reason that they are fad diets is that they will not work for everyone or may not work in the long run.

As a coach working with young girls, you may have to answer questions concerning nutrition and diets. You do not need to be an expert in the field to help your athletes, but you should be aware of the importance of proper nutrition for health and performance. If you are asked a question that you are not sure how to answer, however, do not try to work your way through an answer. Girls aged 7–13 need guidance because they have reached an age where appearance is becoming very important. Therefore, you have a duty to act responsibly and with extreme care when dealing with these problems. Remember the following whenever dealing with a nutritional situation:

- You have a very large influence on the actions of your players, and any comment, no matter how off-the-cuff or innocently it may be intended, is subject to scrutiny by the players. They look to you as an expert, even if you have no background with these issues. Direct the players to proper sources of information, such as their doctors or a certified nutrition professional, if they have questions that you are uncomfortable about or are unsure of.

- It has not ever been established that body size has an effect on soccer performance. There is no ideal body weight or amount of body fat that is related to the success of female soccer players. Casual observation of female collegiate or professional teams reveals that players on the roster have all sorts of body types. If you ever make a suggestion to a player that she needs to address her body weight, you may be setting into motion potential problems in the future. If you feel a need to address this issue with a player, and you feel strongly that you must say something, seek advice from a nutrition professional first.

Although you should not deal with these situations directly unless you are trained in the area, it is important to understand potential issues your players might have. By understanding typical problems and warning signs, you might be able to intervene and help your athletes.

The American College of Sports Medicine (ACSM) has recognized three medical disorders frequently observed with female athletes. These ailments—disordered eating, amenorrhea, and osteoporosis—are identified as the "female athlete triad" because they are interrelated. Individuals who exhibit symptoms of one part of the triad are at an increased risk to experience the others. (Manore and Thompson, in their textbook *Sport Nutrition for Health and Performance,* provide an overview of the female athlete triad.)

The ACSM has issued the following position statement on the female athlete triad:

> The Female Athlete Triad is a syndrome occurring in physically active girls and women. Its interrelated components are disordered eating, amenorrhea, and osteoporosis. Pressure placed on young women to achieve or maintain unrealistically low body weight underlies development of the Triad. Adolescents and women training in sports in which low body weight is emphasized for athletic activity or appearance are at greatest risk. Girls and women with one component of the Triad should be screened for the others.
>
> Alone or in combination, Female Athlete Triad disorders can decrease physical performance and cause morbidity and mortality. More research is needed on its causes, prevalence, treatment, and consequences. All individuals working with physically active girls and women should be educated about the Female Athlete Triad and develop plans to prevent, recognize, treat and reduce its risks.

Disordered Eating

Disordered eating behaviors are those in which the young athletes exhibit abnormal eating patterns. Disordered eating could result from a variety of causes. Two common and very serious eating disorders are *anorexia nervosa* (anorexia) and *bulimia nervosa* (bulimia). Those with anorexia feel that they must be thin and literally starve themselves. They do not get sufficient nutrients in their diet, and the illness is characterized by emotional and physical problems.

A person suffering from bulimia has similar characteristics as a person with anorexia; however, instead of not eating, the bulimic frequently binges and purges. The bulimic will overeat (binge), and then attempt to get rid of (purge) the calories consumed. While many bulimics may vomit intentionally, some might turn to excessive exercise, laxatives, enemas, diuretics, or fasting to purge.

These and other eating disorders can be harmful to the girls' health for many reasons. First and foremost, the athletes will not get the proper nutrition required by their activity level. Second, the emotional problems associated with eating disorders can last a lifetime. As a coach, you should be aware of and on the lookout for these signs of potential eating disorder:

- Prolonged periods of dieting
- Frequent weight fluctuations
- A traumatic stressful event
- Pressure placed on the female to maintain or achieve a low body weight

Amenorrhea

Amenorrhea, or menstrual dysfunction, occurs when the menstrual cycle is disrupted or stopped. Amenorrhea could be the result of inadequate diet (eating disorder), excessive exercise, or a combination of the two. Because excessive exercise can result in menstrual dysfunction, an athlete does not necessarily have to have an eating disorder to experience this situation. However, "the combined effect of diet and exercise appears to have a more negative effect on menstrual status than just exercise or diet alone." There are health-related issues that arise from periods of prolonged amenorrhea. If you feel that one of your players is suffering from this characteristic, consult a health professional for advice and treatment.

Osteoporosis

Osteoporosis is a decrease in bone density that results in the increased risk of bone fractures later in life. Although osteoporosis typically manifests itself later in life, research has found that girls experiencing one or more component of the triad have a greater chance of developing osteoporosis. In addition to relying on adequate nutrition, normal bone density is also dependent upon hormones such as estrogen for proper development. Women who suffer from eating disorders face increased risks of nutritional deficits. Those who suffer from menstrual dysfunction are also at risk, because the disruption of the menstrual cycle results in a disturbance of estrogen production.

It is good that you understand these potential problems so you can act appropriately. Look for the following symptoms in female athletes to help you determine if a potential problem exists.

- Excessive dieting for weight loss, large fluctuations in body weight, or too much weight loss
- Irregular or absent menstrual periods
- Stress fractures, especially recurrent stress fractures
- Self-esteem and mood that appear to be dictated by body weight and shape
- Compulsive overexercise

PROPER NUTRITION FOR THE ATHLETIC ADOLESCENT FEMALE

Female athletes often experience difficulties dealing with body shape and social acceptance. They receive conflicting signals. They want to achieve a certain body type, but their participation in athletics increases requirement for calories. If they have friends who are not participating in athletics, they sometimes struggle because their friends are adhering to one diet, while they adhere to another.

In 1992, the United States Department of Agriculture (USDA) released their Food Guide Pyramid, which was designed to provide guidelines for a healthy daily diet. Dr. Linda Houtkooper has modified the pyramid for athletes as follows:

- Fluids, water
- 6–11 servings of bread, cereal, rice, or pasta
- 2–4 servings of fruit
- 3–5 servings of vegetables
- 3 servings of meat, poultry, beans, eggs, or nuts
- 2–3 servings of milk, yogurt, or cheese
- Sparing use of fats and oils

Of all the items on the list, one of the most important is the proper amount of fluids. During activity the body loses fluid while sweating, and fluid is also lost during menstruation. Make sure your players drink enough water to stay hydrated throughout the day. If they feel thirsty, then they have not had enough water!

Sexual Harassment

In recent years the issue of sexual harassment has received enormous attention. As a coach dealing with young girls, especially if you are a male working with females, you need to be aware of this issue. Even if you are a female working with girls, it is still appropriate for you to be aware of potential problems that might be considered harassment.

According to the Nolo.com legal encyclopedia, a legal definition of sexual harassment is

> Any unwelcome sexual advance or conduct ... that creates an intimidating, hostile or offensive ... environment. In real life, sexually harassing behavior ranges from repeated offensive or belittling jokes to a[n environment] full of offensive pornography to an outright sexual assault.

As a coach, you must be aware that treating your players in any way that offends or intimidates, regardless of your intent, can be interpreted as sexual harassment. Behaviors at practice, at games, or when interacting off the field with your players that includes improper language or improper touching should be avoided at all times. It is possible that actions that you feel are appropriate and innocent can be interpreted as sexual harassment. It is far better to avoid situations that could result in charges of harassment before they occur than to have to deal with problems after they have occurred. This is important because many times actions are mistaken to be negative in intent when in fact they meant nothing.

To avoid situations that could result in charges of harassment, use common sense. In addition, here is some practical advice to help eliminate potential problems:

- Never be in a situation that involves you and a player with no witnesses.
- Never use foul or inflammatory language toward or near your players.
- If a player is waiting on a ride after a practice or game, have at least two adults stay with the child until the appropriate parent or guardian arrives.
- Do not engage with your players in social activities that are not team related.
- While traveling and staying at a hotel or dormitory, if a player wishes to speak with you, make sure witnesses are

present or prop your door open and stay within sight of the hallway.

- Do not call, e-mail, or write to a player in any way that could be interpreted as questionable.

Most of these suggestions are common sense, and all relate to one basic theme that can be applied in most instances when coaching: Prevent problems in the future by acting appropriately now!

Dealing with Parents

A major issue that you will face when coaching is dealing with parents. Parents can either be your greatest allies or your worst adversaries. Some parents will completely base their assessment of your ability to coach upon the playing time that their daughter receives. This is inevitable. The increased media coverage on professional sports has influenced parents in sometimes negative ways. Coaches of professional teams are expected to win games—that is why they are professional. It is common to read about a professional coach who was fired because the team's owner was not happy with results.

At the college, high school, and now club levels, this same attitude is starting to become more prevalent. If results are not satisfactory, the coach is released. If winning is the only priority, this is to be expected. However, if winning is secondary to player development, it should not occur. Unfortunately, the reality is that a major source of problems with parents may be your team's win-loss record.

This problem is worsened with the increased competition for college scholarships and the media attention paid to young athletes. The Little League World Series, which was once covered as a chance for people to see young people playing in a baseball game against another country, has turned into an event that rivals the Major League Baseball World Series. In my community, the Little League team that represents our state in the regional tournament leading to participation in the World Series has its games covered by local radio and newspapers. In girl's soccer, the next step in their athletic career after playing youth soccer is a college scholarship. Pressure from parents for the team to win because they think it will increase their daughter's chances to receive collegiate financial aid often causes problems within the team.

Parental interference also occurs when parents insist upon making their opinions known to the coach. This can be especially frustrating because you are the expert—you are the one who is reading this book, has coached before, has gone to the clinics, and is donating time to help the players improve. This kind of parental interference occurs at all levels. While coaching at the college level, it was not uncommon for me to field several calls throughout the season from parents who were attempting to influence me on matters from coaching to selecting playing time.

Although I cannot predict every situation that you will encounter while coaching, I can offer you some practical advice for dealing with parents. Not all parents are problems. The parents who are not problems, however, will not cause you problems. Probably the problem parents will be limited to one or a few individuals. No matter how frustrating it can be, you must keep in mind why you have chosen to coach. If you reach a point when dealing with the outside issues and interference outweighs the enjoyment and satisfaction you receive while coaching, it is time that you reevaluate your involvement in the game. I hope with this advice that you never reach that point.

- Establish your coaching philosophy, explain it to the parents, and stick with it.
- Establish firm and fair team rules, explain them to the parents, and enforce them.
- If a parent approaches you with a concern, hear the parent out. Most of the time parents have specific complaints that they just want to express to someone. By listening to their concerns, you give them the opportunity to feel that they have expressed their opinions.
- If a parent has a valid complaint, do something about it. Make an appropriate change if you feel, after patiently listening to the parent, that their concern warrants attention. Many times parents will come up with great solutions to problems that you either have had difficulty solving or maybe did not even know existed. If, however, after you have patiently listened to the parent you feel that complaint is not valid, attempt to explain to the parent why you have done what you did and why you made your choice. Many times when the parent sees things from your point of view, they will better understand why a certain action was taken.
- Do not allow parents to bully you. If a parent has a valid complaint, recognize that and make the appropriate changes. If you feel a parent's concern is mistaken, politely explain why you feel your approach is correct. Never, under any circumstances, give in and make a change that you don't agree with just to pacify the parent. This is opening the door to continued interference, because the parent will feel that their opinion meant something.

• If you ever feel that you might be subjected to bodily harm, end the conversation and leave immediately. Alert the proper authorities if you feel that the situation warrants. Always try to have discussions that are potentially problematic with a witness present, preferably an assistant coach or club official.

• Keep lines of communication open. The most important thing that you must continue to do while coaching is to keep the communications open between you and your teams' parents. Make every attempt to greet the parents whenever you can, and use social occasions, such as team parties, to get to know your parents better. Any chance that you have to interact with the parents in an informal manner is a chance to build your relationship.

• Never hold a player responsible for the actions of her parent if the child was not involved. Parents will sometimes approach you and express their concerns without their child's knowledge. There will also be times when parents approach you even though their daughter has tried to stop them. It is not fair to the child if she is held responsible for her parent's actions. As the girls get older, you might establish team rules that concern how issues are addressed. You might want to make it a rule that all problems must first be discussed between the player and the coach. This would be appropriate for players 14 and older. However, most younger players lack the maturity for this rule to be effective.

In my experience, recognizing and making an appropriate change has improved my relationship with the parents, while ignoring invalid suggestions has helped to deter parents from continuing to interfere.

The Stress of Competition

The biggest reason that children drop out of team sports is that they no longer find them fun. There are many reasons why girls may not find soccer to be fun: perhaps they find practices to be redundant, lacking in challenge, and boring.

It is possible however, that the athletes are not having fun because of increased pressure to perform. Coaches with a win-at-all-cost philosophy or overbearing parents can place such a premium on performance that players lose confidence and enjoyment in participating. The stress of competition has made the girls lose motivation for continuing to play.

You can prevent this by adapting a player-development philosophy and by employing positive coaching techniques. Decrease your emphasis on the final score and highlight the importance of doing your best. Get the parents on your side in this manner, because you deal with the girls only at practice and at games. Parents interact with them at all other times. Do your best to explain to parents why a player-development philosophy is important, and help them to recognize if they are guilty of causing undue stress upon their daughters.

SUMMARY

When coaching girls, it is appropriate to use many of the same approaches used when coaching boys. Soccer techniques, tactics, and physical demands are not different for boys and girls, so you need to coach the athlete, not the gender.

Even though boys and girls face the same requirements when playing soccer, however, they are physiologically different, especially as they reach their later teens, and they do exhibit different behaviors. Proper coaching of technique and tactics at an early age can help to increase the players' future chances of success, even as their bodies grow and develop.

Psychological differences between boys and girls seem to result more from society's expectations. But sports participation and the expectations placed upon female athletes are rapidly changing the way that athletes are perceived—for the better.

CHAPTER 4

SOCCER BASICS

SOCCER IS A VERY SIMPLE game: the object is to score more goals than the opposition scores. Getting the ball between the goal posts and into the goal scores a point. To move the ball, players may use any body part except their hands. One player on each team—the goalkeeper—may use her hands while inside the penalty box. At the end of regulation time, the team that has scored the most points wins.

This is the game of soccer in its simplest form. There are factors that make the game more complex, but the popularity of the game lies in its simplicity. When coaching, keep this simplicity in mind. The easier you can make the game for your players, the more they will enjoy playing!

To be an effective coach, you need to have a good understanding of equipment, playing positions, and the rules of the game. The suggestions in this chapter will help you increase your understanding of the game and become more efficient as you coach.

EQUIPMENT

When coaching a soccer team, you will use various pieces of equipment. Your club or league might provide training and match (game) day equipment, or you may have to purchase these items yourself. Or you may find it convenient to own your own equipment. Regardless of your situation, basic soccer equipment will make teaching and coaching easier. Most of the items described in this chapter will be useful during practice sessions, especially if you are not able to practice on a regulation soccer field.

Training Equipment

Some training equipment, such as balls, an air pump, and cones, should be a normal part of your coaching equipment. Others, such as portable goals, can help you become more efficient while coaching, but they are not necessary. The following list has been broken into two parts: required materials and supplemental materials. Required materials are those that all coaches should have to run an efficient training session. Supplemental items are those that are great to have and can prove to be very useful but are not necessary to own.

Soccer Ball   The soccer ball is the most important piece of equipment that you'll need for your practice sessions. The only way that your players can improve their skills and technical ability is to work with a soccer ball. Try to use a ball in every activity you direct during practice.

Soccer balls are made in three different sizes. The size that your players use depends on their age level. Standard ball sizes are 3, 4, and 5, and they vary in circumference and weight. A size 3 ball is the smallest and should be used by players aged 7 and younger (U7s). A size 5 ball is the largest and should be used by players who are 13 and older. Players ages 8–12 should use a size 4 ball. Use the correct ball for the correct ages, not only for skill acquisition and injury prevention, but also to get players comfortable with the ball.

Coaching Tip

Required Soccer Equipment
- Soccer balls
- Cones and markers
- Air pump
- Practice bibs
- Notebook

Often, just like with shoes, parents will purchase an inappropriately sized ball for their daughter. It is very possible that your players' parents are not aware of the differences in ball sizes. Let them know

EVERY PLAYER SHOULD HAVE A SOCCER BALL

Learning and mastering soccer techniques requires repetition, which requires touching the ball. Because you only have practice for a limited time each week, you need to maximize the amount of ball touches per practice. To maximize ball touches:

1. Make sure every player has a ball.
2. Maximize the number of players working on a skill at all times.

When each player has her own ball, more players can be working on individual skills at any given time. You can provide a ball for each player, or you can require each player to bring her own ball. When players bring their own balls, you'll be relieved from filling your trunk with soccer balls, and, more importantly, your players are more likely to practice on their own or with a parent or friend.

There will undoubtedly be times when a player forgets her ball. When developing your team rules, expect this to occur and address the consequences. However, you still need to prepare for this situation, so always bring a couple of extra balls with you. When you provide a ball to a girl who forgot hers, remind her that this should not be repeated, and let her know if it happens again, she will have to sit out of practice. Not letting the players play usually proves to be a good source of motivation.

before the season begins what type of ball should be purchased, and explain the reason in terms of injury prevention and learning.

Cones or Field Markers   After soccer balls, the most vital pieces of practice equipment to own are cones or field markers. You should have at least 24 cones in your equipment bag. Cones are available in many styles and colors. They might lie flat on the ground or stand up. The type you choose is up to you. You can store more flat cones in a space than you can store stand-up cones, and flat cones do not get knocked down.

Cones are used to define the playing areas, known as "grids." Unless you are lucky enough to have your own practice field, you will probably have to share space on a soccer field with one or more teams. Or you might train in an open field or park. In either case, use your cones to define your team's area. The cones also mark boundaries and serve as goals when playing small-sided games. The boundaries not only are references for your players, but also keep others from interfering with your practice.

Cones also serve as a form of pressure on your players. When playing soccer, players experience two types of pressure on the field—pressure from opponents and pressure from the boundaries.

Opponents and boundaries affect the amount of time and space in which your players have to operate. When you restrict the area in which activities occur, you help your players become accustomed to having to control the ball in a defined space, and thus improve their skills. This also allows you to have some control over the difficulty of the exercise.

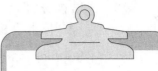

Coaching Tip

Supplemental Soccer Equipment
- Net for a soccer goal
- Portable goals
- Soft balls for heading
- Whistle
- Coaching board/ clipboard

When you purchase your cones, buy more than one color. Use the different colored cones to mark different grids or to serve as goals. For instance, if you have to set up two separate grids, make each a different color. Stay consistent within each grid—that is why you have the varying colors. Or use one color cone to mark sidelines and another to mark goals. Make it easy for your players to identify important areas on the field.

Air Pump Keep an air pump with your extra balls or in your medical kit. Make sure that you have the needles required for inflating the balls. A simple check prior to the beginning of practice to see who needs to have their balls pumped can eliminate headaches on the field. You can also make it the players' responsibility to make sure that their balls are inflated correctly.

Practice Bibs When running a practice session, you will often need to break your team into small groups or into separate teams for scrimmaging. The players should wear different colored shirts to eliminate confusion. You should have at least as many practice bibs as you have players on your team, in two separate colors. For example, when coaching a team of sixteen players, you should have sixteen bibs, eight of one color and eight of another.

Make sure that your groups will be clearly defined when breaking them into small groups. For instance, if you have blue bibs and one of your players is wearing a blue shirt, you will probably want to place her on the blue-bib team. Also, your players will thank you if you wash the practice bibs every once in a while!

Notebook Get a notebook or three-ring binder to keep pertinent information together. If you have injury waiver forms for each player, place them in the notebook so you have easy access to them in case of injury. Keep your practice plans and notes in the notebook. Use the binder to stay organized.

Supplemental Materials

Net for a Soccer Goal   If you practice on a field with a permanent goal, you can use the net during shooting practices. The net can help the players have a reference point while shooting, and hitting the back of the net can help increase your players' confidence and satisfaction. Because many of the activities that you run will involve shooting on a goal, the net can also help keep players from having to chase their balls after they shoot.

Portable Goals   Although not necessary, portable goals, which can be easily transported to and from practice, can be very helpful. Many styles of portable goals are available. They can be full-sized or very small.

Soft Balls for Heading   Heading can be a very frightening technique for young or inexperienced players to perform. Many young players resist hitting the ball with their head or become fearful of the ball as it approaches them. To get your players more comfortable with this technique, you can switch from soccer balls to foam balls or beach balls. As they become less fearful and more confident, you can switch to harder balls.

Whistle   Whistles are great tools for signaling the start and stop of activities. They are listed as supplemental equipment, however, because it is not necessary that you use a whistle. Actually, using your voice may be better training for your players. When coaching during a game, many of your tips will be given during the flow of play. Therefore, your players will have to become proficient at processing information while playing the game. In addition, there are usually many other voices on the field at the same time. You want your team to recognize and hear your voice over and above anyone else's. When you use your voice instead of a whistle during practice, you are training the players to respond to you.

However, a whistle is good to have in your practice bag in case you get called into refereeing. It might also be useful if you scrimmage at the end of practice. If you want to be most effective, however, try not to use a whistle during practice. Use your voice instead.

Coaching Board or Clipboard   A coaching board or clipboard can be useful when diagramming a play to your team. You might want to show your players where they should run during a goal kick, or maybe you'll want to explain to an individual which areas of the field she should be working within. Use the coaching board to help your players see what you are explaining to them. Pen and paper work just as well, so use a clipboard if it's easier and if you feel it will be beneficial.

Match Day Equipment

On match or game day, you will use many of the same items that you used during practice. You might use your cones and bibs during the warm-up. It could happen that your team and the other team wear the same colored uniform, and someone will have to change. Have your practice bibs on hand in case this happens. You may also want to have a clipboard or coaching board to diagram plays and positions.

Some coaches like to keep stats during games. Many standardized statistical forms are available, or you can design your own. You might want to ask a parent or assistant to help you collect statistics, especially if you want to keep records that are more complicated than just shots, saves, and goals scored. Many times parents are happy and feel honored to help collect these numbers.

PLAYERS AND POSITIONS

There are many different ways to organize a soccer team on the field. In general, however, there are four basic positions in soccer: goalkeeper, fullback, midfielder, and forward (see figure 4.1). Think of each position as a player or group of players who work in different areas of the field. Goalkeepers play in front of your team's own goal. Fullbacks play in front of the goalkeeper. Midfielders are positioned ahead of the fullbacks, and forwards are stationed in front of the midfielders.

The *goalkeeper* is the only player on the field who may use her hands during the flow of play. Goalkeeping is a specialty position, requiring different techniques than those used by field players. A goalkeeper must, however, be comfortable using her feet as a field player would, because there are instances when she may not use her hands. Goalkeeper techniques include catching, punting, and throwing the ball. Some leagues do not use goalkeepers in the younger age groups. This is because many youngsters have not yet developed sufficient coordination to fill the needs of the position.

Fullbacks play in front of the goalkeeper. While their position is primarily defensive, fullbacks can and should get into the attack.

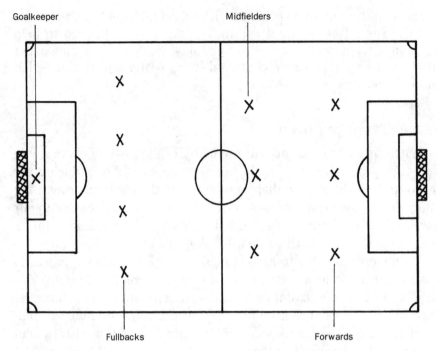

Goalkeeper   Midfielders

Fullbacks   Forwards

FIGURE 4.1
Soccer field showing different positions

Teams usually play with three or four fullbacks spread out along the width of the field. Although fullbacks might spend a majority of their time defending, they should be capable of shooting on goal and making accurate passes.

The *midfielder's* job is to control the middle of the field. Midfielders frequently help move the ball from the back of the team to the front or from one side of the field to the other. Midfielders need to be able to attack and defend equally as well. Midfielders will also cover more area on the field than most other players will, so they need to have stamina. Teams play with three, four, or five midfielders spread out from side to side. The central midfielder or central midfielders (if using more than one) are the core of the team. Because they are stationed in the center of the team's formation, they are usually involved in all action, both attacking and defending. The central midfielder is usually the team's most skillful player.

Forwards, or *strikers*, are the players at the front of your team. Their main job is to set up and score goals, although they do have defensive responsibilities. Forwards should be the players who are hungry to score goals, but also realize that they have to help when your team is on defense. Teams usually play with two or three forwards.

Table 4.1 outlines the basic positions in soccer and their typical requirements. These are the positions you will fill when determining what formation or system your team will use. However, you may have more than one player in a position, or you may not have anyone play certain positions. For example, you might have two central midfielders, or you might only play with two forwards. The positions in soccer are much more like those of basketball or hockey than of softball or volleyball: Consider the positions to be locations of players relative to their teammates but non-confining to a certain location on the field.

11 Attack and 11 Defend

Many times players can be heard saying that they either play defense or attack. The stereotypical job of a fullback is to defend, while that of a forward is to attack. Players and parents sometimes fall into the notion that the fullback's *only* job is to defend. It is not uncommon to watch a youth game and see the fullbacks standing on the top of

Table 4.1 Soccer Positions and Their Characteristics

Left Forward	**Center Forward**	**Right Forward**
Good left foot	Shoots with either foot	Good right foot
Speedy	Good ball control	Speedy
Strong shot	Likes to play 1 V 1	Strong shot
Left Midfielder	**Center Midfielder**	**Right Midfielder**
Good left foot	Good passer	Good right foot
Speedy	Good ball control	Speedy
Can cross well	Likes to run	Can cross well
Left Fullback	**Center Fullback**	**Right Fullback**
Likes to defend	Likes to defend	Likes to defend
Good header	Good header	Good header
Accurate passer	Strong leg	Accurate passer
Goalkeeper		
Good with hands		
Fearless		
Likes to jump		

WHO SHOULD PLAY WHERE?

Follow these strategies when selecting positions:

1. **Let the player select her own position.** Ask your player what position she plays. Many times, especially if the player has had some experience, she might have settled into a favorite position or two.

2. **Rotate positions.** Have each player play every position, by rotating game by game or half by half. Give each player enough time to become acquainted with each position. If your team does not have a regular goalkeeper, or if you have many players who would like to play in goal, rotate them so everyone gets a chance. The rotation strategy is good to use with inexperienced players and to help your players understand the different roles of their teammates.

3. **Let players gravitate to their positions.** Many times players will naturally move toward a position that best suits their playing ability and desires. Play a scrimmage game during practice, but don't assign positions. Or play a four-a-side tournament during practice. Instead of coaching, stand on the side and note who goes forward, who stays back, and who sets up the play. Your players may be telling you indirectly whether they prefer to play forward, midfielder, defender, or goalkeeper. This is a great method to use when you are unsure of where to place a certain player.

4. **Assign specific positions.** Assess your players and place them where they can best use their strengths and hide their weaknesses. Use the characteristics of each position to help determine appropriate places for your players. Use this method to help your players determine which positions are better for them.

their own penalty box while the ball is on the other side of the field. They have been instructed that their job is to stay there to keep the ball from going into the goal. Unfortunately, when this happens, they become spectators when their team has the ball.

As a coach, you need to preach the concept that when your team has the ball, everyone is on the attack and when your team doesn't have the ball, everyone is on the defense. Players and parents need to realize and be taught that defenders do more than stand in front of their own goal, and forwards do more than just score goals. If you are an experienced coach, you undoubtedly have had the opportunity to watch or coach a forward who thought that her only job was to attack. When your team has the ball, she is very active. As soon as your team loses the ball, she stops. You can help to change this mentality by encouraging everyone to attack and everyone to defend.

Of course, this does not mean that when your team has the ball, every player runs forward. What it means is that each player and position has a role when your team has the ball and when your team does not have the ball. For instance, your forwards' job when your team has the ball is to create scoring opportunities. When your team loses the ball, your forwards become your first line of defense. Think about it: Is it easier to score after winning the ball in front of your own goal, or in front of the other team's goal? By encouraging the concept of everyone attacking and everyone defending, you also help your players understand how to play other positions, and thus help in their development as complete players.

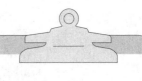

Coaching Tip

Prior to the age of 10, players should not be specializing in goalkeeping. If they are, they also need to be able to play without their hands because of the rules pertaining to a pass back from their own team.

THE RULES OF THE GAME

There are seventeen rules, or laws, of soccer. The laws of the game are simple and are pretty consistent from level to level when eleven players are playing on each team. Many organizations, including U.S. Soccer and AYSO, advocate modifying the rules for younger players. In addition, many leagues have determined their own modifications.

Get a copy of the official laws of soccer. You can find books at bookstores and soccer specialty stores. You can also download a copy of the official rules from the Fédération Internationale de Football Association (FIFA) Web site (www.fifa.com). Many of the laws, however, are not of interest to the average youth soccer player or coach because they deal with technicalities. Rather than explain every law as it appears in the official rulebook, this book discusses specific rules that you will probably find more pertinent to your coaching.

11-a-Side Rules
The Field of Play

A soccer field, or *pitch*, consists of a marked rectangle with goals on either end. The size of the field can vary, but there are specific minimum and maximum dimensions listed in the laws of the games. All pitches are divided in half with a half-line, which is important during kick-offs and when determining if a player is offside.

Although the total size of the pitch may vary, the inner marked areas all have measurements in one-to-three ratios, as shown in figure 4.2. In other words, the three important areas—the goal area, the penalty box, and the goals themselves—all are rectangles with one dimension three times the length of the other dimension. The goal area and penalty box are three times as wide as they are long. The goal is three times as wide as it is high. Interesting, and also easy to remember!

The *goal area,* which is part of the penalty box (see below), is the small box directly in front of each goal, measuring 6 yards long and 18 yards wide. The goal area is important for two reasons:

1. All goal kicks must be taken from somewhere inside the goal area.

2. If a foul occurs in the goal area that results in an indirect kick for the attacking team, the ball must be moved outside of the goal area before the kick is taken.

The *penalty box* is the large box in front of each goal. It measures 18 yards long and 44 yards wide. Sometimes the penalty box is

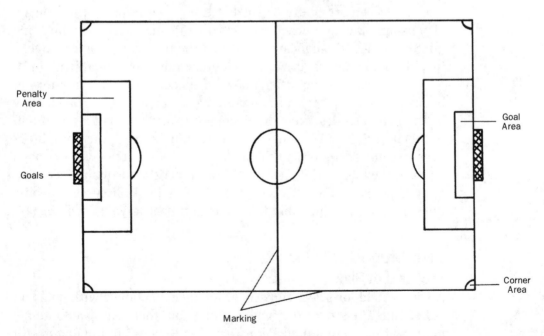

FIGURE 4.2
Areas of the field

called the 18-yard box because of its dimensions. The goalkeeper may handle the ball while within the penalty box as long as she adheres to specific goalkeeper rules. Once the goalkeeper leaves the penalty box, she becomes a field player and may not handle (use her hands on) the ball. If the defending team commits a foul resulting in a direct free kick inside the penalty area, the attacking team is awarded a penalty kick. Indirect free kick fouls are handled the same as if they occurred outside of the box.

The *goals* on a regulation soccer pitch are 8 feet tall and 24 feet wide. Younger players often play with smaller goals to account for their size differences. A team's own goal is the goal that they are currently defending.

Ball In and Out of Play

All lines and markings on a soccer field are considered to be a part of the area they define. In other words, the sidelines and endlines are a part of the field. For a ball to be considered out of play, it must completely cross the line, whether on the ground or in the air. A ball touching a line is considered to be in play. (See figure 4.3.)

When determining if the ball is in or out of play, all that matters is the ball itself. A player touching the ball is not taken into account. For instance, a player might have one foot out of bounds but kicks the ball while it is in bounds. The ball is still considered to be in play.

The fact that the ball must completely cross the line is also important when scoring. For a goal to count, the ball must completely cross the goal line. A goal occurs when the ball leaves the field of play between the goal posts and underneath the crossbar. If the defending team stops the ball before it completely crosses the goal line, no goal has occurred.

Educate your players and parents about this rule. They need to understand this difference in soccer from other popular sports that they may have played. The safest course of action is to instruct your players to keep on playing until they hear a whistle.

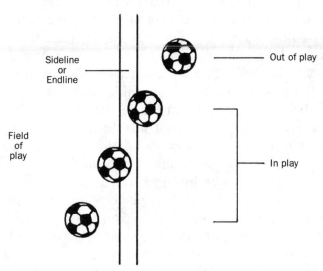

FIGURE 4.3
In and out of play

Players' Equipment

A soccer uniform consists of a shirt, shorts, long socks, and shoes. The socks should completely cover the player's shin guards, which are the only mandatory piece of equipment for all players. The players may not, however, wear anything that poses a danger to themselves or others.

The goalkeeper must wear a jersey that distinguishes her from her teammates, the referees, and her opponents. Many styles of fancy goalkeeping jerseys exist, but a different colored shirt or practice bib will also suffice. The goalkeeper's jersey should also be different from the opposing goalkeeper's jersey. Many times the referees are willing to overlook this rule because it is rare that the two goalkeepers will be playing near each other. The key is that everyone needs to be able to recognize the goalkeeper at all times. Goalkeepers may also wear gloves and long pants to help protect from injury, but these are not required.

Offsides

The offside law is probably the most confusing rule in soccer. It is confusing because a player can be in an offside position but not be called offsides. It is also confusing because the location in which your players might be caught offsides is always changing. Many leagues do not use the offside rule for younger players.

To better understand the offside rule, there are two things to take into account: its purpose and the difference between being in an *offside position* and being *offside*. The offside rule was created to eliminate teams stationing attacking players in front of the opponent's goal for the entire match. If there were no offsides, teams would place a "cherry-picker" down the field. Once they got possession of the ball, they would try to make a long pass to the advanced player, who would be in a good position to score. The game of soccer would change significantly, resembling a big tennis match. Many teams would stop playing short passes and instead rely on a long passing game. Soccer would become a game in which success was highly dependent upon how far players could kick the ball.

It is possible for a player to be in an offside position without being called offside. Think of it this way: A player is in an *offside position* if she is nearer to the opponent's goal than to (1) the halfline, (2) the ball, and (3) the second-to-last opponent. A player is *offside* if she is in an offside position and is involved in the play. In other words, a player can be in an offside position at any time, but should not be called offsides until the ball is passed to her. The determination of offsides occurs when the pass is made, not when the player receives the ball. In other words, as long as the player remains in an onside position at the time that the ball is played by her teammate, she can run into an offside position to receive the ball without penalty (see figure 4.4). If a player is guilty of being offside, the defending team receives a free kick from the spot of the infraction (where the offside player was located).

When determining the second-to-last opponent, all players, including the goalkeeper, are taken into account. In almost all cases, the goalkeeper stays near the goal, so the second-to-last opponent is usually the deepest field player. Imagine a line running from sideline to sideline that goes through the last defender. This is the line of offsides. If a player is even with this line or if she is nearer to her own goal than this line, she is not in an offside position. This line moves with the second-to-last opponent.

Explain to your players the offensive and defensive implications of offsides. From an attacking standpoint, your players need to know that they can push up to deepest fullback and remain onside. They also need to know that once the ball is passed, they can run forward without being offside. Defensively, the players need to realize that if they move toward the half-line, the opponents must move with them or they might be offside. If your fullbacks stand very deep in their own half and never come forward, the other team can push up to them and have an advantage.

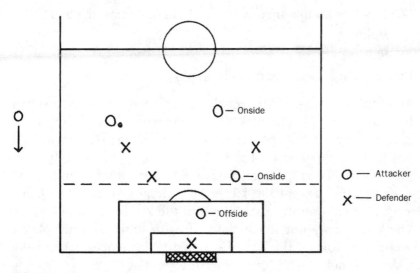

FIGURE 4.4
Various onside and offside positions

Explain also that a player can be in an offside position without being called for offsides. The assistant referee will raise the flag to signal if a player is in an offside position, but the referee can decide that the offending player was not involved in the play and not call the foul. Players should never stop playing when they see a flag—only when they hear a whistle.

Fouls

There are many fouls that might be committed, but there are only two awards to the team against which the foul occurred: a direct kick or an indirect kick. A *direct kick* is a free kick with which the attacking team can score directly. Unless occurring within the penalty box, the kick is taken from the spot of the foul. The player taking the free kick can kick the ball directly into the goal. The defending team may be no closer than 10 yards from the spot of the ball. Many times, defenses will place players to block the kick, forming a wall to help defend the goal. As long as the wall is no closer than 10 yards to the ball, it is legal. There are 10 fouls that result in a direct free kick:

1. Kicking an opponent
2. Tripping
3. Jumping
4. Charging an opponent
5. Striking or attempting to strike an opponent
6. Pushing
7. Tackling an opponent without first contacting the ball
8. Holding
9. Spitting
10. Touching the ball with your hands

Any foul occurring in the penalty box that would have resulted in a direct free kick for the attacking team results in a penalty kick. During a penalty kick, a shooter gets a one-on-one opportunity to score against the goalkeeper. The ball is placed on the penalty spot, which is 12 yards from the goal. No players from either team may be in the penalty box except the kicker and the goalkeeper. The goalkeeper must remain on the goal line until the kicker has touched the ball. The kicker may not touch the ball again until another player touches it. Therefore, if the ball hits a post and bounces back to the kicker, she may not touch it until someone else has.

Indirect kicks occur from the spot of less serious fouls. A foul committed inside the penalty box that results in an indirect free kick remains an indirect kick from the spot of the ball. On an indirect free kick, a second player other than the kicker must touch the ball before it may score. The touch could be from a teammate or opponent. If the ball goes into the goal without being touched by a second player, there is no goal. Instead, the defending team gets a goal kick. The 10-yard rule for the defending team applies also to indirect kicks. Fouls that result in an indirect kick include:

1. Dangerous play (any action that the referee feels is dangerous to the guilty player or those around her, like a high kick)
2. Obstructing an opponent while not playing the ball
3. Blocking the goalkeeper when she has the ball

Most infractions limited to goalkeepers also result in indirect free kicks, including:

1. Holding the ball for longer than six seconds
2. Handling a ball that a teammate has passed back with her feet
3. Handling a ball that she has dropped without it being touched by another player
4. Handling a throw-in from her own team
5. Wasting time

Restarts

There are four basic ways that the ball is put into play: a kick-off, a throw-in, a corner kick, and a goal kick. For all kicks, the 10-yard rule for defenders applies, just as during direct and indirect free kicks.

A *kick-off* occurs at the start of each half. It also occurs after a goal has been scored. During a kick-off, each team must stay within its own half. The kick-off occurs at the half-line and must move forward. The team kicking-off at the beginning of each half is decided during the pregame coin flip. After each goal, the team that has been scored upon restarts the game with a kick-off. Teach your players to use the kick-off to make a pass to a teammate, rather than kicking it to the other team like in football. Your team should use the kick-off to maintain possession.

A team restarts the ball with a *throw-in* when the opponents have last touched the ball before it goes over a sideline. Any player may complete the throw-in. The player taking the throw-in must have two hands on the ball, have both feet in contact with the ground when releasing the ball, and must use a motion that brings the ball from behind to over the head (see figure 4.5). The player must use both hands equally—the ball should not have any sidespin. Any infractions on a throw-in result in a throw-in being awarded to the other team.

A team earns a *corner kick* when the opposing team last touches a ball before it goes over their endline. Any player on the team takes the kick from the corner nearest to the spot that the ball left the field.

A corner kick is considered a direct kick—a player can score directly on the kick without the ball being touched by anyone else.

A *goal kick* occurs when the attacking team last touches the ball before it goes over the opponent's endline. The defending team restarts the game with a goal kick, which occurs from anywhere within the goal box. Once again, any player can perform the goal kick. It is advisable, however, to have your goalkeeper take the kick. No one may touch the ball until it leaves the penalty box, and no opposing players may be in the penalty box when the kick is taken.

FIGURE 4.5
Example of a throw-in

Referee and Assistant Referees

The *referee's* job is to enforce the rules of the game and to ensure the safety of all participants. The referee has sole discretion to decide when a foul has occurred and to assess the required penalty.

The two *assistant referees* help the referee during the match. Assistant referees are often necessary because the pitch is so big. (In the past, assistant referees were referred to as linesmen.) The assistant referees stand on either sideline and use flags to signal the referee whenever the ball leaves the field of play. When the ball goes out of bounds, they signal who should be awarded the ball. The assistant referees also use their flags to signal to the referee whenever they see a foul that the referee may not have seen, or when a player is in an offside position.

In most cases, the referee will award a free kick to the team against which the foul was committed. The referee may also "award" a yellow card or red card to a person committing a more serious offense. A yellow card is a warning. A player or coach may receive a yellow card if he or she is guilty of unsporting behavior or if he or she shows dissent to the referee or assistant referees. In general, a player will receive a yellow card whenever she does something that the referee feels is very inappropriate.

A red card is more serious than a yellow card. A person receiving a red card is expelled from the game. If a player receives a red card, she cannot be substituted, and her team must play with one less player than the opposition. Red cards are automatic if a player receives a second yellow card in the same game. They will also occur if the referee feels that the player is guilty of an action serious enough to warrant immediate expulsion, such as fighting, using foul and abusive language, or committing a very violent foul. The rules

LETTER OF THE LAW VERSUS SPIRIT OF THE LAW

When deciding whether to call a foul, referees will often try to judge if the spirit of the law was broken. If they feel that the reason for the rule was not broken, even if the actual rule was, they might not blow their whistle. For instance, the rules state that no players may touch the ball with their hands except the goalkeeper. If the ball does touch a player's arm or hand, but the referee feels that it was unintentional, the ref might say, "Play on," and let play continue.

Rules are made to place the team committing the foul at a disadvantage. The referee may let play continue if it is felt that the foul would give an advantage to the defending team. If a player is dribbling the ball and gets pushed, the referee could call a foul. However, maybe the player regained balance in time to keep control of the ball and has dribbled past the player who pushed her. In this case, calling a foul would help the defending team to recover and, thus, would penalize the team that should have gotten the advantage. This also could occur when a player is offside. Perhaps the player that is offside does not receive the ball, but rather the pass is intercepted. Instead of stopping the game, the referee may allow play to continue because the ball was turned over.

Sometimes calls seemed delayed. This may be because the referee waited a second or two to see if the attacking team still had the advantage. Educate your players and their parents about this concept. Players or parents often get upset because they feel that a foul occurred that was not called. But it could be that a foul would have helped the other team, and so the referee let play continue.

state that anyone who deliberately uses her hands to stop an obvious goal or who deliberately takes down a player on a breakaway to goal has also committed a red-card offense. Players, coaches, and spectators may receive yellow and red cards, and most leagues also have additional punishments for those receiving repeated cards.

Modifications for Younger Players

Many leagues and organizations adopt modified rules for players of younger ages. Most of the modifications deal with field size, goal size, and number of players. The number of players is reduced to encourage more players actually touching the ball during a game. Other rules, such as offside or the use of goalkeepers, might be eliminated.

Most of the rule changes result from practical common sense. Young players are often just learning the rules of the game and have a difficult time keeping them straight. A league might have a guideline that after a foul, the referee should stop and explain to the player why a foul was called. Sometimes, players might be given a second chance to perform a throw-in after an illegal throw. Consult your league for the modifications that you will be playing with during the season.

WHY CHANGE THE RULES?

Some people are opposed to changing the rules for younger players. They might have concerns that players should learn the proper rules from the beginning, or that the game is not really soccer if the official rules are not followed. If you keep in mind your player-development philosophy, however, you can easily see that rule modifications are necessary and important.

The laws of soccer state that each team shall have 11 players on the field. However, all players derive enjoyment from kicking the ball. When each team has 11 players, there is one ball for 22 athletes. The opportunity for each player to touch the ball is greatly reduced. By having fewer players on the field, the amount of touches per player increases, as do the chances for individual success and satisfaction.

Rule modifications are necessary because there are certain things that children have difficulty accomplishing. Changing the field size, eliminating goalkeepers and/or offside, and changing how the ball is put into play make the game easier for young players. The idea is to foster success—that is what makes the players want to come back!

SUMMARY

One of your first jobs when coaching young players will be to introduce your players to the game. Many players will be experiencing soccer for the first time, and you will be teaching them everything they need to know. Much of your teaching will occur during training sessions, so you must have the equipment necessary to run efficient practices.

Like most other sports, soccer is a game involving positions. Teams can adopt many different formations on the field, but in general, player positions fall into four basic categories: goalkeeper, fullback, midfielder, and forward. Although each position has different roles and is exposed to different situations, you need to teach your players that no matter what their position may be, when their team has the ball, they all attack. When the other team has the ball, they all defend. There is no position in soccer that only does one or the other.

5

THE PILLARS OF THE GAME

TO BE AN EFFECTIVE coach, it is vital to have a basic appreciation not only for the rules of soccer, but also for the components of soccer, or the pillars of the game. When you are coaching soccer, you will address four basic areas: technique, tactics, physical fitness, and psychology. Technique, tactics, and physical fitness all involve the physical approach to the game, while psychology involves the mental aspect. These four categories are the pillars of the game, because no matter what type of strategy or system of play you choose to utilize, you will always be concerned with each. This chapter provides an overview of each component. Later chapters will discuss each area in greater detail.

When determining which of the components you will address during each practice session, you must take into account the ages and stages of development of your players. Six-year-olds look, think, and act differently than eight-year-olds do. As the players grow, their needs and capabilities change. This chapter addresses the different characteristics of players as they progress from the U6 to the U12 age groups, along with how these differences apply to you as their coach.

Finally, to be efficient when working with your players, you need to use effective teaching methods. You need to have an understanding of how people learn. The last part of this chapter deals with the teaching process and how you should present and reinforce the concepts of soccer to your players. The teaching process is the same no matter what age you are working with—the complexity of the subject is what needs to be varied.

THE FOUR PILLARS

Although different groups can play soccer using different strategies, technique, tactics, fitness, and psychology are always present. These four components are really the components of any sport. What makes the style of play different is the emphasis placed on each component. For instance, an activity like running a marathon requires efficient running (technique), deciding when to pick up your pace and when to reserve energy (tactics), the ability to cover 26+ miles (physical fitness), and the ability to maintain focus for a couple of hours (psychology). The fitness and psychological aspects play a greater role in

DIFFERENT BUT THE SAME

If you follow soccer on an international level, you might notice that teams from different parts of the world use different strategies or styles. A team from Europe might use different strategies than a team from South America. Here are a couple of possibilities for why they use different strategies:

1. **Climate.** In places where the climate is warm, it might be necessary to adopt a style that allows players to conserve energy. Instead of playing with long passes (which forces players to do a lot of running), a short passing game might be emphasized so that the ball does much of the work. Conversely, in countries that are cold and wet, certain field conditions might make short passing or passing on the ground difficult. Teams might emphasize passing in the air or long passing to cover more area without the ball hitting the ground.

2. **Tradition.** It could be that certain styles of play were developed in the past, and because young players tend to emulate the older or professional players, they attempt to play in the same way. The tradition of play then gets handed down from generation to generation and becomes a trademark of that country. The Norwegians play a long ball style, which highlights long passes and tall players, which might be a case of current players emulating players from the past.

No particular style is best. In the past ten years, teams representing all parts of the world using many different styles have been successful. No matter which style is used, the components of the game are always involved. One style may stress fitness, while another style focuses on tactics. Regardless, the player's technical abilities remain the most important component.

a runner's success than the technique and tactics used, but nonetheless all of the components are involved.

In soccer, the most important element is technique. Techniques are the skills of soccer. Without technique, it does not matter how well you make decisions (tactics), how long you can run (endurance), nor how you deal with the stress of competition (psychology). When working with players of all levels, technique must be the emphasis of your coaching.

Technique

Soccer techniques, or the skills used to play the game, are the fundamentals of soccer. Every technique used by your players falls under one of the following eight categories: juggling, dribbling, passing, ball control, heading, finishing, tackling, and goalkeeping. Your priority as a teacher should be your players' mastery of technique.

Without technique, mastery of the other components becomes useless. All eight techniques involve at least one player *and* a soccer ball. Your team maintains possession of the ball using technique. If your team cannot keep the ball, it has very little chance of scoring. In addition, players derive enjoyment from their contact with the ball. If your team does not have the ball very often, your players could become frustrated. It is a waste of time to develop strategies of play or to work on your players' fitness levels if they are not able to pass, dribble, or control the ball. Once your players become familiar with the basic techniques of the game, more emphasis can be placed on the other components.

There are eight basic areas of technique, and there are a variety of uses and ways to perform in each area. Therefore, the total amount of soccer techniques is unlimited. Following is a description of each technique, along with some of the different manners in which it is performed:

- **Juggling.** A player juggles a ball when she repeatedly keeps the ball from hitting the ground by using various parts of her body. She juggles with her feet, thighs, chest, head, and shoulders. A player starts juggling by lifting the ball off the ground without using her hands (a technique called a pickup). Although juggling may not occur often during a game, players juggle to increase their ability to control the ball, so it is worthwhile to practice.

- **Dribbling.** Dribbling involves keeping possession of the ball with your feet. Various surfaces of the feet are used, including the inside, outside, instep, and soles. Players dribble to go past opponents (beat them), to go away from opponents or sidelines, and to move quickly in open spaces. Each type of dribbling requires a different technique. Dribbling technique also involves body feints and tricks to fool opponents. Players use their heads, shoulders, legs, and small touches of the ball to fake opponents by beating them with a dribble.

- **Passing.** Players pass the ball to move it from one part of the field to another. There are various types of passes. Short passes usually remain on the ground, while long passes may be on the ground or in the air. Balls might be driven, lofted, or curved (bent). Each type of pass requires a slightly different technique.

- **Ball control.** Receiving the ball is important for maintaining possession. When players control the ball, they may use various body parts, such as their feet, thighs, chests, and heads. They might also use different surfaces of each body part. For example, a player might use the inside or outside of her foot when receiving a pass on the ground, or she might use the instep or sole of her foot when receiving a ball out of the air.

- **Heading.** Players head the ball with their foreheads. Heading may be used for attacking or defending. A player might try to head the ball into the goal or to pass it to another player. Soccer players also use their heads defensively to hit the ball away or to clear the ball. Players who are standing, jumping, or diving might attempt headers.

- **Finishing.** Players finish to score goals. Finishing might be better described as a pass into the goal. The techniques used when finishing are very similar to those used when passing. Players must work on striking a ball that is rolling, bouncing, or in the air. A ball struck just after it bounces is called a half volley, while a ball struck out of the air is considered a full volley. In addition to mastering how to finish a ball that is rolling, bouncing, or in the air, players also need to work on finishing balls coming toward them, moving away from them, or coming from the side.

- **Tackling.** Players tackle the ball to dispossess another player. A tackle occurs when a defending player knocks the ball away from an opponent who is in possession. In soccer, a player tackles the ball, not another player. There are several ways to tackle the ball, including the poke tackle, the block tackle, and the slide tackle. When a player tackles the ball, her intent should be to get the ball away from an opponent, but not necessarily to win the ball herself. Tackling is the only technique that is used solely for defensive purposes. You would never tackle a teammate.

- **Goalkeeping.** Goalkeeper is a specialty position, requiring work on specific techniques used only by that player. Goalkeepers need to work on catching balls coming at them. Balls could either be on the ground or in the air. Air balls could be below the waist, chest level, or over the head. Balls could also be directly at them or to their side, requiring a dive to make the save. When the goalkeeper has the ball, she needs to be able to get it to one of her teammates by punting, throwing, or rolling the ball.

There are an endless number of techniques that you can work on with your players. Practicing each technique once a season, however, is not sufficient for the players to master them. Training needs to be repeated and reinforced from practice to practice and season to season. Incorporate the other components of soccer into your practice sessions as necessary, but always include practice of technique.

Tactics

Soccer tactics are the strategies that players and teams use to play the game. When you teach tactics to your players, you are actually teaching them how to make correct decisions. During a match, a player needs to make many decisions, usually with very little time to think. Teach and reinforce tactics by coaching exercises that require the players to make the same decision, or face the same problem, repeatedly.

IS HEADING DANGEROUS?

There is no doubt that injuries may occur when an object strikes a person's head. If a ball were coming at a player at a very high speed, any contact with the head could be similar to a person being punched. When younger players play soccer, however, it is highly improbable that a ball could be struck hard enough to replicate this action.

As a percentage of people playing soccer in the world, the number of people with heading injuries is very small. Most that have been reported are to advanced players who have been playing for a long time and are heading balls that are traveling much faster than what young players would experience. Explain to your players, and if necessary, to their parents, the need to head the ball correctly. Heading is part of the game of soccer, and if performed correctly, the chances of injury are greatly reduced.

Attacking Tactics Teams use attacking tactics when they have the ball. Attacking tactics include individual attack (1 against 1 or 1 V 1), small group tactics (2 V 2, 3 V 3, etc.), and large group or team tactics (7 V 7 up to 11 V 11). Some of the concepts to address include taking players on (beating them with a dribble), combination play (two or three players using passes to move the ball), and team shape (how your team is spread out and deployed in the field).

Defending Tactics Individual defending tactics involve jockeying (or moving with) the player with the ball, or marking (guarding against) a player without the ball. When working on jockeying, you will have to address how and when your players should tackle the ball. Small group tactics when defending include teaching players how to cover for each other and how to balance the field to make sure that opponents far away from the ball are marked. Large group defending tactics focus on how your players are positioned and how they work together when the other team has the ball.

Coaching Tip

Technical mastery takes years for a player to perfect. Be patient when teaching your players. Many times, the work that you do with players one season does not reveal itself until a few seasons later.

Both attacking and defending tactics include individual, small group, and large group practices. When working with your players on tactics, focus more on individual and small group tactics than on large group tactics for both attacking and defending. The reason is threefold:

1. Individual and small group tactics are less complex and simpler to understand than large group tactics.
2. By mastering individual and small group tactics your players will inherently begin to develop large group tactics.
3. No matter how many players are on the field, when analyzing play you can always reduce the big game to a 1 V 1 or 2 V 1 situation involving the ball. The team that wins more of the 1 V 1 or 2 V 1 situations throughout a match is more likely to be the winner of the game.

Physical Fitness

Many people associate fitness with the ability to run for a long time (aerobic fitness); soccer players actually have a few more requirements.

Think of fitness, or fitness level, as the ingredients necessary to move and perform the techniques and tactics of soccer for an extended period of time. There is no doubt that aerobic endurance is important, but there are some other items that players need to be concerned with. These include:

Cardiovascular Endurance Cardiovascular endurance is involved with the body's ability to get oxygen and fuel to muscles *and* to take away waste products from the muscles. There are two types of endurance in soccer.

1. Aerobic endurance allows a player to compete in a full game without slowing or tiring. Aerobic endurance involves the body's ability to process oxygen. A marathon runner needs a high level of aerobic endurance. Aerobic endurance can be improved by performing an activity continuously for at least 30 minutes.

2. A person uses anaerobic endurance when she performs a series of sprints or repeated efforts of high intensity followed by rest. Anaerobic endurance involves the body's ability remove waste (lactic acid) away from muscles. A sprinter needs a high level of anaerobic endurance. This type of endurance can be improved by performing repeated high intensity bouts of activity for about one minute followed by a short recovery period. Research has shown that soccer players need both types of endurance.

Strength Strength is the ability to move a mass. Sometimes the weight is the player herself, and at other times the weight is another person. Although strength is not an absolute requirement of soccer players, it can definitely help to foster success. Strength can be increased with resistance training.

Flexibility Flexibility is the ability to move a joint through a range of motion. Greater flexibility allows for greater movement and decreases the chance of injury to joints and the surrounding tissues. Increasing flexibility can also lead to improved agility and balance. Help your players increase flexibility by doing static stretching exercises.

Agility Agility is the ability to change direction while maintaining balance. Players need agility in order to fake other players and to stay with opponents who try to beat them. Any activity involving quick and repeated changes of direction will help to improve agility.

Speed Pure speed is how fast a player can move from point *A* to point *B*. Pure speed is genetic—you either have it or you don't. A

USE TRAINING TIME WISELY!

Without a doubt, fitness is important for soccer players. Most people relate fitness level to endurance level, while in fact other components are more important. If your team trains two or three times per week, there is little that you can do to improve your players' cardiovascular endurance levels. In fact, research has shown that aerobic training with prepubescent children results in little improvement, simply because their bodies have not yet fully developed and don't respond to endurance training like adults do. If you are working with younger players, chances are that they are just as active, if not more, when they are away from practice, so they do not need to work on fitness during your valuable training time.

   If you want to work on a component of fitness with young players, work on agility. This will help them master their ever-changing bodies and become more comfortable with the ball.

player can improve pure speed by working on running form and leg strength, but unless she was way out of shape, improvements will be small.

Psychology

The psychological component of soccer concerns how you deal with your players and how they deal with each other. It concerns how they react to the pressures and stress of competition and to the success and failures associated with competing. One of the most successful ways that you can motivate your players is by dealing with your team as individuals, all of whom have different needs.

   One method used by coaches and athletes to address the mental aspects of competing involves *goal setting*. You can use individual goals and team goals to both motivate and encourage your players. You might choose to give each individual a different goal during a game or practice, or you might come up with a team goal during a game. Use the goals to help the players experience success, and make them specific. For instance, you might give one of

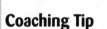

Coaching Tip

Organize activities so that many groups are working at the same time. Endurance is improved with constant motion. The motion does not have to be running laps, but instead could be running with the ball.

your players the goal to use her left foot at least five times during a practice. Instead of imploring the player to work on her left foot, the goal instead plays on the psychological aspect of that player and her desire to make you happy. If she meets the goal, congratulate her.

AGE-GROUP CONSIDERATIONS

Although the components of soccer can be summarized in four categories, each category has many details associated with it. Part of being an effective coach requires that you teach correct and appropriate topics to your players. Of course, the skill and experience level of your players will have an effect on what you choose to work on. However, for younger players, their current stage of development, rather than their experience playing soccer, should be the main influence upon your choices.

If you have coached before, especially if you have worked with a variety of age levels, you have probably found that certain activities work well with one age group but do not fare well for another. Sometimes an activity may be too simple or too complex for a team. However, most of the time you can know beforehand what will and will not work based on the physical, mental, and emotional characteristics of the players. Table 5.1 summarizes the age group needs for each of the components of the game. Use this to guide you as you plan your training topics and practice sessions.

Under 8s

Under 8s (U8s) are five-, six-, and seven-year-olds. They are often just beginning to learn the game. Soccer might be their first organ-

Table 5.1 Summary of Age Group Needs

	Technique	Tactics	Fitness	Psychology
U8	****	*	–	****
U10	****	**	–	****
U12	****	***	*	****
U14	****	****	**	****

**** Very High Priority
*** High Priority
** Medium Priority
* Low Priority
– Not Important

ized activity. These players are still growing, and any injuries near joints require special attention because the growth plates may be involved. U8s are less efficient aerobically and in regulating body temperature than adults are, so if you are working on a hot day, provide frequent breaks to the players. These players have a difficult time concentrating and performing more than one task at a time, and they have a difficult time determining appropriate time and space relationships. This means that when teaching the players, break actions down into a sequence of simple tasks. For instance, to an adult, controlling the ball, looking at the goal, and finishing in one fluid motion might not seem to be a difficult movement, but to the U8, this is actually a group of tasks that need to be completed one after the other. The difficulty in performing this exercise is that the players are being mentally overloaded.

U8s associate playing well with trying hard. If they tried their best, then in their minds they did well, regardless of the actual outcome. They are very susceptible to being hurt by negative comments because they strive for approval from adults and friends. Most players this age have one very good friend, so partner activities are very appropriate during practice. Finally, while these players might understand that they are on a team, they are not able to conceptualize a league. It is just too complex for them. They play soccer because they want to—it is fun. Therefore, your focus should be on playing games that encourage the use of simple techniques. Players in this age group also respond well to make-believe. By naming or creating games involving fantasy play, like dinosaurs or racing cars, you can use their imaginations to keep them on task.

Under 10s

As the players move to U10, they become capable of understanding more complex concepts. They are now able to complete a series of tasks in order, such as controlling the ball and scoring a goal. At this age, the players also begin to become capable of thinking ahead, which means that they can be introduced to basic tactics. Because the players are very enthusiastic and want to learn, technical work should be your greatest focus. At this age girls are starting to enter puberty and enter a period of accelerated growth.

Because U10 players are becoming more advanced mentally, they are capable of working in small groups. Techniques and tactics can be introduced and explained in soccer terms rather than in fantasy terms. U10 players start to understand what will work and what will not, although many times they are not quite sure why. U10 girls demonstrate an increased level of self-responsibility, and therefore rules about proper dress and proper gear to bring to practice can be used and enforced.

Under 12s

Most of your under 12s will be in the middle of their pubescence. Growth spurts and physical changes will often make players very different from season to season. It is vital that you continue to focus on technique at this level. Although the players may have learned or mastered a specific technique in the past, their changing body size may require them to relearn the skill from year to year. Flexibility, strength, and endurance are areas that can be improved with training. Near the end of this age group, many players drop out of soccer, so it is crucial that you maintain an awareness of possible overuse and burnout.

U12s can think in abstract terms and address hypothetical situations. This means that you can begin to work on tactical concepts, because the players are becoming able to make decisions based on forethought. Popularity among peers is also becoming an issue as the players begin to spend more time with their friends and less with their parents. You can use peer pressure to help when enforcing team rules by using positive actions of teammates as examples.

Under 14s

Although they are not yet adults, U14s can begin to be addressed as adult soccer players. Most have completed puberty, so fitness may need to be addressed. Technique should still be emphasized, but practice can be more tailored to focus on tactics, including small group, large group, and situational tactics (like dealing with a corner kick). U14 players are capable of being presented with choices and should be able to select the appropriate response.

Burnout, overuse, and peer pressure are evident in the U14s. When working with this age group, training still needs to be fun. You can, however, adjust training to address the situations in the game—the players will derive their fun from performing correctly and successfully.

When you have difficulty motivating a player or team, you can appeal to their sense of responsibility to their teammates. Relationships with you and others on the team are very important to these players, and many times the threat of losing their rapport with others will result in a change in behavior.

THE TEACHING PROCESS

When learning a new skill or method, correct repetition is most important. As you probably know from experience, a physical skill, like kicking a ball, or a mental skill, like reading or writing, is mastered by performing the skill over and over until mistakes are reduced or eliminated. You probably were not consistently able to perform the skill correctly at first. Instead you made mistakes and then reduced the number of mistakes until you mastered the skill. Even then, you still made mistakes, but they were few and far between. The same will be true when you teach a new concept to your players. It is okay if your players make many mistakes when learning a new concept or skill. Your job is to help the players eliminate mistakes so they can become better players.

When teaching a skill or concept, you need to follow a logical teaching process. In this process, you will demonstrate the skill and then let the players practice while you detect and analyze correct and incorrect performance, provide feedback about their mistakes, and allow them to practice over again. The process repeats until the skill is learned (see figure 5.1).

Following is a more detailed explanation of the teaching process.

1. Demonstrate. Show the players the correct action. A picture is worth a thousand words, and explaining a skill with words can be confusing. The demonstration does not need to be at game speed, and it can be broken down into parts, but it should be executed so that the players have a clear idea of what they need to accomplish.

2. Practice. Once the demonstration is complete, allow the players to practice the skill. Many mistakes will occur, especially if the skill is new or complex. This is okay! Players learn not only by seeing what a correct action looks like, but also by recognizing how an incorrect action looks and feels. During this phase, you should be analyzing performance to determine what type of feedback you are going to provide.

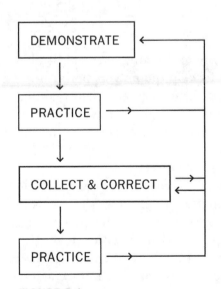

FIGURE 5.1
The Teaching Process

WHAT IF I CAN'T DEMONSTRATE?

Many coaches have little or no experience in actually playing, but they do understand how a skill or action should be executed. There are many ways that you can efficiently demonstrate a skill without having mastered it yourself:

- **Demonstrate slowly or show only parts of the skill.** When showing a technique, break it down into parts and show it slowly. Build up to a correct performance. For example, one of the most important skills in soccer is controlling a pass. In the game, most often a player will be moving when she receives a pass, and a defender may be trying to get the ball away from her. You do not need to replicate all of these situations when demonstrating—it is sufficient for you to stand still while showing your team how to control the ball. After your players have mastered controlling the ball, have them start the movement.

- **Have a player demonstrate.** Many times it is effective to let your players perform the demonstration while you explain the action. This is especially effective if you have a player who has already mastered the skill, or if the action seems difficult and the players need to be convinced that they can actually perform it. Learning among individuals occurs at different rates, so the chances are good that you will have some players who can perform skills better than others.

- **Have an assistant coach or "guest expert" demonstrate.** Ask an assistant coach or a guest to demonstrate. Your players might have older sisters who play, or the local high school or college team may be able to provide a guest coach. Investigate within your community to find creative solutions.

3. Collect and correct. This is where teaching occurs. Mistakes are identified and feedback is given to help the players perform the skill correctly. In addition, correct performances are identified and the players are told or encouraged when they perform well. Corrections should be positive and should explain how to perform the skill correctly. It does not help a player to be told what she is doing wrong without an explanation of how to perform correctly.

There are three different methods to collect and correct, and many successful coaches use a combination of all three. The first is to use large group correction or reinforcement. If many players are repeating the same mistakes frequently, it is most efficient to give corrections to the entire group. Single out one or two major mistakes that are occurring, and show how they can be corrected. Once again, this involves demonstration. Remember that mistakes may occur because the skill is difficult, or perhaps because the explanation or initial demonstration was not clear. You might also single out one or two players who are performing the activity correctly. Have them demonstrate for the team, and then recognize them in front of the group when they perform well.

You can also use small group correction or reinforcement. Sometimes a few players may be having the same difficulty, or maybe your practice is organized so that many small groups are working independently. In this case, instead of stopping everyone, stop just the smaller group and make corrections or reinforce actions while the rest of the team continues to work.

Finally, you can use individual correction or reinforcement. This is a good technique for helping players improve more quickly and also for satisfying the players' need for recognition. This could involve calling a player over to you, or walking through the team and calling out directions to players by using their names. This is especially effective and important when developing relationships with girls.

No matter which method you use, remember that reinforcing correct performance will always be more effective than correcting incorrect performance. The athletes will have a clear picture or feeling of correct performance when it occurs. Even if the skill is performed incorrectly, recognizing a small portion that was correct will help the player enjoy partial success.

When practicing, how long you let mistakes keep occurring depends on your players and the types of mistakes they are making. If the mistakes are easily correctable, go ahead and correct quickly. If they are small or occurring infrequently, let the players play. Remember that they did not come to training to hear the coach—they came to play. (I know that might be painful to the ego, but it is the truth!)

4. Practice again. After collecting and correcting or reinforcing, the players need to be given the opportunity to practice again. Steps 3 and 4 may be repeated, or you might have to go back to step 1. Either way, repetition is involved, which is how learning occurs. When teaching, try continually to ask yourself whether the activity is too easy or too difficult and if the activity applies to the game of soccer. Monitoring the level of difficulty of the activity will help you determine whether any adjustments need to be made. The adjustments might include making the exercise easier or more difficult to challenge the players and allow success. Optimal learning occurs when the players are challenged enough to make performance difficult, but not so overwhelmed that performance is impossible. The players will lose interest if the activity is too easy or too difficult.

Many techniques and tactics must be introduced or trained in a way that encourages success for the players. But because these techniques are complex, you can introduce them in a manner that is not game-like. For instance, a dribbling move where a player uses a fake to go past an opponent should be introduced without opposition, but obviously it needs to be mastered against an opponent to be useful in a game. Therefore, once the basic movement is mastered, the challenge needs to be gradually adjusted to match the level experienced during an actual game. This might occur over a series of practices rather than in one practice. If the players are not given a chance to train in gamelike situations, they should not be expected to play as they did in practice.

SUMMARY

Soccer requires the mastery of technique, tactics, physical fitness, and psychology. While these components may have different levels of emphasis for different age levels and in different parts of the world, they are always present in the game. Focus on technique no matter whom or what level you are coaching. You can always adjust the requirements to challenge players of any level.

When selecting appropriate training activities, you need to take not only the skill level of your players into account, but also their stage of mental, physical, and emotional development. By selecting appropriate activities, not only will you be more efficient in your coaching, but also your players will be more motivated to perform.

No matter what you choose to teach, you need to follow a progression. Learning occurs through correct repetition and through the elimination of mistakes. Your feedback while working with the players is your main job as their coach—you are their teacher.

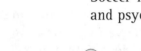

Coaching Tip

Drills imply that players are repeating the same task, without making decisions. Exercises imply that both physical activity and decision making occur. Soccer is a player's game. Allow players the freedom to make decisions, even when an exercise allows only certain decisions to be made.

6

PLANNING A TRAINING SESSION

OF ALL THE DUTIES and roles that you fulfill when coaching, the task that you will do more than any other will be planning and running training sessions. It is in these training sessions that you will do practically all of your teaching, because you can completely control the environment of the sessions. You can manipulate the simplicity and complexity of each task so you can control the success rate of your players. You can stop the players at practice when they make mistakes to provide them with the vital feedback that is necessary to learning.

Because training sessions are so important to the development of your players, you need to approach each session with a plan. You should try not to wing it at a practice session or to run a training session without first thinking about what you would like to accomplish. When organizing a session, make sure that your practices involve a progression from simple to complex. You should organize economically; that is, your chosen training activities should involve as many components of soccer as possible at all times.

In addition to planning individual sessions, you should develop a long-term plan. This plan should reflect your priorities, philosophies, and goals for the team. You may plan for the entire season, or maybe for each week at a time. Whichever method you choose, your planning should be based on a progression from session to session and from week to week to best develop your players.

There are many different activities that you can use to teach your players. No matter which activities you choose, however, make sure that they are developmentally appropriate for your team. Activities that are too easy or too difficult may not be effective and could result in boredom or frustration. The appendix provides some sample training sessions for the various age groups discussed in this book. Use these examples as models when planning your practices.

DEVELOPING A GOOD TRAINING SESSION

When you plan a practice for your team, you need to keep a few items in mind. By following the simple suggestions that follow, you will find that your training sessions become much more effective at bringing about improvement in your players.

Select a Theme or Topic

All effective practice sessions have a specified theme. The theme of your practice defines the purpose for that day's training. It keeps your practices aimed at improving a single facet of the game. By selecting a theme for each of your training sessions, you simplify learning and allow your players to focus on improving a single activity.

All of the activities undertaken in your practice should be related to your theme, and your coaching should be geared toward introducing, correcting, and reinforcing the performance of the chosen topic. This does not mean that you cannot make coaching points about other topics. Your main focus, however, should be on analyzing and correcting action related to your current theme.

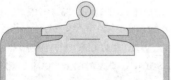

Coaching Tip

At the beginning of each practice, tell your team the theme for the day. This will help them understand the day's focus.

Allot Enough Time for Each Activity

Learning occurs through repetition. When you select activities, make sure that you allot enough time for each exercise. In general, each activity should probably last at least 10–20 minutes to be effective. Just as players might become bored if you plan too few exercises, they might become confused by trying to get through too many activities and might not master the task at hand. It is okay to plan for too many activities, as long as you are willing to be flexible when running your training session. If a game is working well and the players are staying on task, consider skipping the next activity.

Arrange Activities from Simple to Complex

Effective learning best occurs when your players are first required to carry out a simple action. After they realize some success, increase the demands of the action to approach those required during a match. Remember that if your players consistently practice a move or skill without opposition, it is doubtful that they will be able to perform it correctly during a game. When you teach in a simple to complex manner, you teach in a progression. Your activities build upon each other, moving from basic to gamelike within the training session.

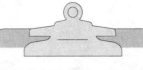

Coaching Tip

When first introducing a technique, the fundamental stage might involve little or no movement. When trying to perfect a technique that has already been introduced, the fundamental stage might begin with movement.

There are different progressions used, depending on what you are teaching. When working on a technique, such as dribbling or passing, the basic progression is as follows:

1. Fundamental. Make your initial exercise a fundamental exercise, or an exercise that involves little or no movement and is used to perfect a basic action. For example, when teaching a dribbling move or feint, have players work with a ball that is either still or moving slowly. When working on passing, have players stay in the same location or move slowly. Simplify the movement as much as possible.

2. Game related. Once your players have mastered the fundamental stage, move on to activities that are game related. A game-related activity, such as keep-away, allows players to perform the technique under increased pressure, but with less pressure than they would experience in a live game. Game-related activities incorporate movement and frequent repetition of the topic.

3. Game conditions. This, the final stage in the progression, is when you have players perform the skill as it would be executed during a game. Game-conditioned activities involve opposition and should give players something specific to accomplish. These activities are not necessarily exactly like a game. You should alter the rules to provide players with incentives to perform the desired action. For

instance, if the topic of the day is heading, then perhaps the incentive is a player receives a point each time she heads the ball during the game. Players are encouraged not only to score in the regular goal, but also to try to head the ball.

Tactics, on the other hand, can be divided into two broad categories: attacking and defending. The type of tactic is obviously defined by one simple fact—which team has the ball. If your team has the ball, then your team should use attacking tactics. If your team does not have the ball, then they should use defending tactics. Therefore, the tactical progression starts with who is in possession of the ball.

When you are teaching tactics, as opposed to techniques, your focus is on the decision-making aspect of the game. Once again, you should use a progression in which activities move from simple to complex.

1. **Possession.** Use a possession-oriented activity to begin teaching your tactical theme. Depending on your theme, your focus will either be on those who have the ball (attacking) or those without the ball (defending). If your theme is attacking, base points on how your team should act to keep the ball. If your theme is defending, coach your players either on how to keep the attacking team from getting past them or on how they can work to win the ball. You might place restrictions on your players to allow successful decisions to be made. For instance, if working on defending, your team needs to learn how to win the ball. If your attacking team is not good at keeping the ball, however, the defending group could be successful without carrying out the desired actions. By giving the attacking team more space or more players to help them keep the ball, you can make the defending challenges more realistic.

2. **Play to one goal.** The object of soccer is to score a goal. Therefore attackers could be considered successful if they score, and your defenders could be considered successful if they keep the attackers from scoring. Create activities to reinforce your tactical topic using a goal.

3. **Play to two goals.** Once your players have worked on making correct decisions in activities that are not yet gamelike, you need to progress toward gamelike conditions. Playing games with two goals places your team in situations that replicate the game. Once again, instead of scrimmaging, play conditioned games that bring about the action that you would like the players to work on. For instance, if your topic is 1 V 1 attack, you could require that anytime a player has the ball, she must attempt to dribble past an opponent before passing or shooting.

Make Your Training Economical

All of your training activities should be economical. In other words, your activities should involve at least two of the components of soccer at all times. Economical activities make the best use of your practice time and generate better and more efficient learning and development for your players.

Exercises that involve at least one ball, or better yet as many balls as possible, are probably the most economical training you can employ. If you are working on technique, the players will have to choose when to perform the action or what to do once the action is completed, which is tactics. If you are working on tactics, the players will probably have to dribble, pass, receive, head, and/or shoot the ball, which is technique. Even if you feel that you need to work on fitness, have players perform the activity while in possession of a ball. Players will improve not only their fitness level but also their ability to maintain control of the ball while working.

Coaching Tip

All exercises should involve shooting on goal, so use a goal whenever possible—even if the tactical topic does not involve shooting.

EFFECTIVELY ORGANIZING THE PRACTICE

When setting up your training session, there are a few essentials that can help you remain organized. By keeping the following points in mind, you will find that your sessions are more effective and provide an excellent learning environment.

Coaching Tip

Requiring each player to bring her own ball to practice ensures that all players will have the opportunity to work on individual skills.

Use Grids

The most common organizational tool for coaching soccer is the use of grids (see figure 6.1). Grids are marked areas that define the working space for a game or activity. The use of grids is important for a few reasons:

1. Grids replicate the soccer field. Although an actual soccer field may be much larger than the grids that you use during training sessions, the common property of a grid and a soccer field is the presence of a defined boundary. Grids force players to respect that the sidelines are also a form of pressure.

2. Grids automatically supply pressure, because they limit the amount of space in which players can perform.

3. Grids keep players organized. The use of grids will allow you to have multiple groups working at the same time while remaining independent from each other. This will help you run more efficient training sessions while keeping players from becoming confused with other groups.

The size of each grid is one of the variables over which you have complete control. Use grid sizes that allow for successful and safe repetition. Change grid sizes to decrease or increase the amount of pressure. A larger grid size may decrease the pressure on an attacking group because they have more space to work with, and thus more time to make their decisions or complete their actions. On the other hand, a larger grid will increase the amount of pressure on a defending group because they must cover more space and have less time to make decisions.

Although there is no one specific grid size that needs to be used, it might be helpful to keep the following in mind when you are unsure of an appropriate starting size.

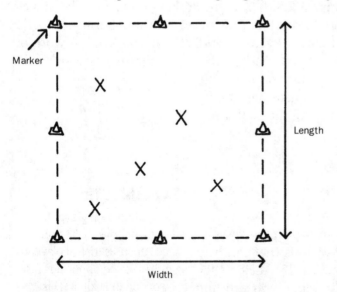

FIGURE 6.1
Example of a practice grid

1. Make your grids rectangular. Even if the sides are only one yard longer than the ends, a rectangular grid mimics a soccer field.

2. Allow each person in the grid about a 5-yard-by-5-yard area to work in. If your activity involves four players, your grid should have at least four 5-yard-by-5-yard areas, or a grid that is at least 12 yards by 10 yards (to keep it rectangular). Trial and error will help you determine appropriate sizes that sufficiently challenge your players.

When forming your grids, avoid using common boundaries between two or more areas. In other words, do not build grids upon each other unless the common border is actually part of a larger grid. When two adjacent grids share a similar sideline, injuries could occur if players from the adjacent areas collide with each other. In addition, what is out of bounds for one area is in play for the other—another potential injury source.

If you are lucky enough to practice on a marked field, use the lines to help you build your grids (see figure 6.2). If possible, set your grids in the place on the field where the practiced action is likely to occur. For instance, if you are working on beating players in a 1 V 1 situation, placing your grid at the top of the penalty area replicates the spot on the field where your players will likely attempt this action.

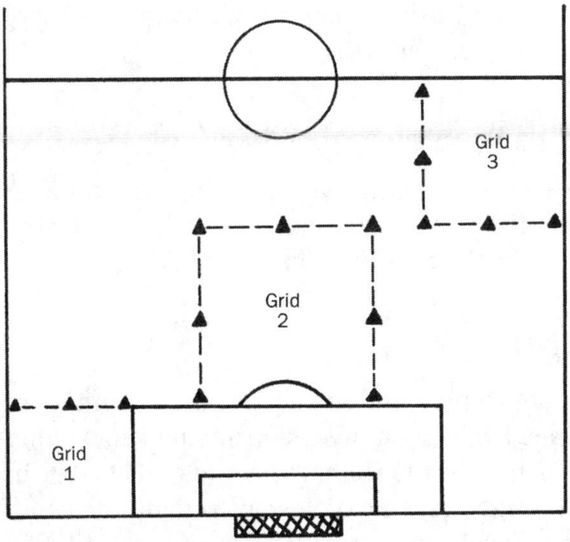

When you set up your practice area, make sure that it is safe and free of any holes, ruts, or other irregularities that could cause injury to your players. If the training area that you have been assigned contains any of these features, set up your grids to avoid these places. If that is

Coaching Tip

Consider setting up multiple grids side by side so you can stand and see all grids at one time. Make sure you allow for space between the grids, and try to stand so you are facing the sun and/or with the wind at your back.

FIGURE 6.2

Example of grid use on lined field

impossible, but you feel that the spot is not dangerous enough to warrant a complete change in practice location, mark the hole with a cone to remind your players of its place. Sprinkler heads are common obstacles that may also need your attention.

During your training session, make sure you keep the grids free of any extra equipment. An unused ball or discarded warm-up jacket could cause an injury if a player inadvertently stumbles or trips over it. Place extra balls outside of the grids, and have your players keep any jackets or sweatshirts alongside their bags or water bottles.

When working with grids, take into account the set-up time between activities. When choosing your activities, design your practice areas so you can avoid lengthy resets between exercises. For example, if you are going to finish your training session with a 4 V 4 game on a 20-yard-by-30-yard field, and all of the other activities need grids that are smaller, set up your game area at the start of practice with smaller grids inside the larger area (see figure 6.3). That way, when you get to the final game, all you need to do is pick up the cones defining the smaller areas.

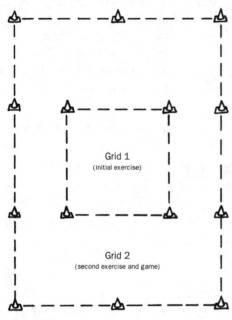

FIGURE 6.3
Example of economical grid set-up

Assign Bibs at Start of Practice

By assigning bibs at the start of practice, you minimize the number of times you need to change the groups working together during your session, and you increase the time available for playing soccer.

PLANNING A SPECIFIC SESSION

As you determine your practice plan and implement the session, plan for a specific length of time. Each training session should last as long as an actual game. There is no truth to the idea that more is better. In fact, by planning long training sessions, you may actually do more harm than good, because your players may get burned out and begin to dislike attending practices.

When you state that practice will end at a given time, remain true to your word. Just as it might be frustrating to you when your players arrive late, it is just as frustrating to players and parents when your practices repeatedly run overtime. If you are in the middle of a game and your practice is nearing its ending time, do not hesitate to stop before you complete all your activities. If you stop practice when it is most fun, your players will leave excited and eager for the next practice.

One thing that you might incorporate into your planning is alternate planning, in case players are missing or late to practice. Be prepared for an uneven number of players. Plan activities that use individuals or small groups so it will be easier to deal with situations in which you have a different amount of players than you expected.

Your entire training session should follow a progression, starting with a description of the theme, followed by a warm-up and then your main activities, and finishing with a final game. After the final game, end your practice with a cooldown to wrap up and summarize the day's work.

Coaching Tip

If you assign a certain color bib to half of your team at the beginning of practice, you can complete all of your activities with clearly defined groups, and you won't have to reorganize your team for each activity.

Announce and Explain Your Theme

Begin each practice with a simple, short, to-the-point explanation of the day's theme. Your explanation might be as simple as a single sentence. For instance, "Today we are going to work on passing with the inside of the foot." By stating your theme, you immediately prepare players for the content of practice, and you help get them mentally prepared for the upcoming activities.

Coaching Tip

Be flexible! You should always have a practice plan, but do not be a slave to it. Make adjustments and abandon activities that are not working. Allow players to continue working on an exercise that is going well. As long as you try to end with a game, you will probably run a successful practice.

Start with a Warm-Up

Your initial activity should be a warm-up, which is used to prepare the body for physical activity and should involve movement. If possible, make your warm-up activity reflect the theme for the day. For instance, if your topic is dribbling, use a dribbling game or work on a ball feint. Your warm-up could be the fundamental portion of your progression and should last 15–20 minutes.

It is also okay to have the players perform an activity that will put them in the mindset of soccer, even if it is not related to the day's topic. For example, even though your theme might be passing, you could do a warm-up consisting of dribbling to prepare your team for the upcoming practice. Or you might want to develop a warm-up that is the same for every practice to get your players into a routine. No matter which approach you choose, make sure your warm-up involves a gradual increase in intensity, is related to soccer, is eco-

AVOID THE THREE L'S

When coaching, do your best to avoid the three L's—lines, laps, and lectures. By reducing and eliminating the three L's, you will increase the efficiency of your training sessions.

- **Lines.** Any activity involving lines of waiting players means that players are not working. Try to avoid activities that have lines of players at all costs. Most activities that you see or use that include lines can probably be changed to reduce or eliminate the lines. For example, instead of having your players line up so they can shoot one at a time at a goal, make multiple goals using cones and have many players work at the same time.

- **Laps.** For some reason, coaches everywhere start their practices by having their teams run a lap. Who knows why this has come about, but in any case, the players are not increasing their soccer skills when they run laps around a field. The only thing that they might increase is their fitness level, but even this is doubtful because most of the players will run at less than the necessary effort for improvement. Running one lap is not going to increase cardiovascular fitness. Eliminate laps and replace with individual ball work to increase productivity.

- **Lectures.** As much as we might like to think so, the players did not come to practice to hear coaches speak—they came to play. And the game of soccer is the best teacher. If you find yourself talking to your players about a skill, tactic, or situation for longer than one minute, you are probably speaking too much. Work on getting your point across clearly, with a minimum of words.

nomical, and involves some sort of stretching or flexibility exercises after some movement has been completed.

Plan the Main Activities

After the warm-up, use the middle of practice to address and develop a progression based on your theme. Your main activities should take up about half of your practice time, and may be one, two, or three exercises that you feel best address the topic of the day. Choose exercises that increase in complexity and approach gamelike situations.

You'll perform most of your coaching duties during the main activities. Your job is to demonstrate the activity, let the players perform, analyze to determine correct and incorrect performance, provide feedback, and let the players practice again. Analysis and feedback may occur repeatedly. Once you feel that the players have performed the activity to your liking, or if you feel that the players are having difficulty staying on task, you should move to the next activity.

For younger players (U8), you might find it difficult to keep the players on task because of their short attention spans. If so, a useful approach is to select a few activities that can be repeated one after the other, two or three times. For example, have the players play game 1, then game 2, and finally game 3. Then repeat the cycle. In this case, you will actually play a total of six games. But because a small amount of time is spent with each game, the players are more likely to maintain their attention. If your players are staying occupied with a certain activity, however, stay with that game.

When correcting mistakes, it is good to use the freeze method to provide feedback. When you coach with the freeze technique, you require each player to stop, or freeze, exactly where she is so you can point out a mistake or a correct action. The idea is to provide a concrete example in which the players can see and understand why a particular action was right or wrong. For example, if a player makes a pass that is intercepted, you could freeze the play to show what would have been a better choice. You are providing

Coaching Tip

If you decide to repeat a series of exercises, use similar playing areas and involve similar numbers of players to reduce organization time between activities.

a perfect picture so that when players are in the same situation in the future, they will be better prepared to make the correct choice.

When using the freeze method of coaching, it is vital that you remember two important issues. First, for players to best realize why a mistake was made, you need to recreate the situation exactly as it occurred. If players move into different locations, the point that you are trying to make may not be apparent. Explain to your players prior to the session that when they hear you say "Stop" or "Freeze," they need to remain where they are. If you have to "rewind," or have the players move back to where they were when you identified the mistake, then do so.

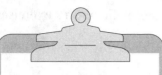

Coaching Tip

Placing restrictions on players gives attacking players the chance to experience success while encountering opposition. Use restrictions so players experience success, but strive to reduce restrictions so players practice under realistic pressure.

The second issue concerns stopping play too often. As you coach, you will find that you could probably stop every play to point out a mistake. If you stop play too often, players will become frustrated, and learning will stop. Freeze play when necessary, but do not overdo it. You can usually figure out when you are stopping play too much by the reaction of your players. In general, you should freeze play less and less as the exercise progresses.

When designing your activities, increase the pressure on your players to approach that of gamelike situations. The only way that you can find out how well players will be able to perform the theme or topic during a game is to observe them in exercises that reflect the demands of the game.

Set Up a Final Game

Your final game, which should take up the last quarter of your session, should be one that reflects a real game of soccer. The final game should involve two teams, each trying to score in a goal. During the initial part of your final game, include a condition that brings out the theme of your training sessions. For example, if your theme is dribbling, you could require the players to touch the ball at least three times before passing, or you could reward extra points if a goal is scored by dribbling past an opponent. No matter what condition you choose, however, make sure that it is realistic to the game. For instance, if your topic was heading, a requirement of having to score with a head ball could make a player on a breakaway do something

WHAT DOES *PRESSURE* MEAN?

When coaches manipulate the pressure on their players during a training session, this means they are manipulating the mental stress that players are experiencing. That is a different type of pressure—one that you should try to reduce and eliminate. Rather, increasing the pressure on players refers to the increasing complexity of performance. You can increase pressure by

1. Decreasing time to perform

2. Decreasing space to perform in

3. Manipulating time and space

Becoming proficient at a skill or technique means that a player is able to perform the action correctly. During a game, however, players will experience situations during which they have little time or space within which to perform the action. This will require quicker decisions and better ball and body control. As a coach, you can change the pressure by manipulating time and/or space, perhaps by making the grid a different size or by changing the amount of opponents. Any restrictions on the opponents (i.e., not allowing them to tackle the ball) can also be manipulated. Decrease pressure to make the activity easier. Increase pressure to make the action harder. It should always be your goal, however, to get to a point where there are no restrictions on the opponents—as is the situation during a game.

that she would not do during a game. In general, conditions that reward are better than conditions that require because the players may still choose to complete the action in a gamelike situation, rather than do something that is unrealistic.

Set up multiple small-sided games to allow more players the opportunity to touch the ball and perform the theme. Many times, a 3 V 3 (three versus three) tournament to end practice is an effective way to let many players touch the ball while incorporating a competitive aspect.

No matter how you choose to implement the final game, allow the final portion of the game to be played without conditions (free play). For this last, condition-free portion of the game, assess the efficiency of the session. Are players attempting to perform the theme of the session? If they are, are they being successful? If not, why not? If you see the topic being performed during free play, you can assume that you were successful at teaching and that there was a transfer from the session to the game. If players are not performing the theme or are performing the action unsuccessfully, then either the players are not comfortable at performing the action during gamelike situations, or perhaps you need to rethink your progression. Either way, this analysis will provide you with valuable information about future training sessions.

End with a Cool-Down

The final part of practice should be the cool-down, which brings the body down from a state of high activity to rest. Cool-down activities should last 5–10 minutes and should consist of light running and stretching. It is at this time that flexibility can be enhanced. Use the cool-down period to make any final announcements pertaining to future practices or games.

LONG-TERM PLANNING

In addition to developing a plan for each practice session, it is a good idea to make a plan of attack for the entire season. Season-long planning need not be a complex chore. Before or shortly after your first practice, jot down some of the concepts that you would like your team and players to become proficient with by the end of the season. Many of these goals will depend on your team's age and developmental level. Once you have an idea of what you would like to focus upon, you can develop a plan that addresses the long-term needs of your players.

Set up your long-term season plan by following a progression so that sessions can build upon one another. For example, if your players cannot dribble well with the ball, it would be unwise to try to teach them advanced dribbling feints at their first training session. Instead it would be appropriate to introduce this more complex topic after a basic session or two on dribbling.

There are two approaches that you can take when making your season-long plan. The first pre-plans the entire season. With this plan, you will know exactly what you will work on during each week. The second approach plans the season in phases. The season could be broken up into a first and second half, or maybe even week-by-week phases. When you plan in this manner, you need to keep a record of what you have worked on already so you remember what has been addressed.

Coaching Tip

If your players do not play 11 V 11, then you should never use that set up during practice. If they do play 11 V 11, then spending a little time at the end of one of your weekly training sessions should be enough to work on their positioning.

Planning the Entire Season

If you choose to plan for the entire season, you should do so before the first training session. There are two ways to use this method: the complete season plan and the partial season plan. For both methods, assume that you are planning for an eight-week season during which you have two practices per week.

In the complete season plan, you plan the entire season without regard to match results. With this approach, you'll decide in advance what your team will work on for the whole season. Player performance during weekly games will not be used for planning. Your plan is driven, instead, by the fact that you want your players to learn specific things by the end of the season. This is a good approach when working with U8 players or with those who are playing soccer for the first time.

If you have sixteen training sessions to plan, you can address the eight techniques of the game and perhaps a basic tactic (see table 6.1). Remember that working on a technique once will not make it permanent, so you will need to repeat each technique throughout the season. Also keep in mind that techniques can be broken down into smaller components. It's possible to spend sixteen sessions working on variations of a single technique! When working with younger players, expose them to as many techniques as possible so they have a chance to experience the many different requirements of the game.

Notice in table 6.1 that the techniques have been repeated, but a slightly different focus has been used for each session.

Another method that you could use is a partial plan. With this approach, you plan for the season all at once, but only for one session a week. The other session is left open for you to decide immediately

Table 6.1   Example of a Complete Season Plan

Week	Session 1 (Tuesday)	Session 2 (Thursday)
1	Juggling	Dribbling
2	Passing	Receiving (ground)
3	Shooting	Heading
4	Dribbling (running with ball)	Passing (long passing)
5	Receiving (out of air)	Shooting
6	Heading	1 V 1 attack
7	1 V 1 defense	Dribbling
8	Passing	Shooting

prior to that session what would be most useful for your players (see table 6.2). You could choose something that they did not do well during their game, or you could repeat a topic that needs more work.

When you plan for the entire season, whether completely or partially, you provide your team with a framework to work within. You know in advance what your focus will be for the week, and you ensure that you will cover all of the technical areas of the game. In addition, planning early can help reduce the week-by-week planning. A drawback to this method is the assumption that your players need equal amounts of work in all areas, rather than extra work in one area or another. Just as with training sessions, however, you should not be a slave to your preparation. Your plan is just a guide to help give you a logical approach to the season. Change your plan at any time to better conform to the needs of your team.

Planning Phases of the Season

The other option is to break your season into periods, or *phases*. When you plan for phases of the season, instead of making a plan that lasts the entire season, you plan for a short period and then reevaluate your team prior to planning for the next phase. If you have an eight-week season, you might divide your season into two portions—the first half and the second half. Your first plan would be for the first half of the season. You would then plan the second half as you near the end of the first part of the season. Analysis of your team's strengths and weaknesses would provide you with new priorities for your second plan.

Table 6.2 Example of a Partial Season Plan

Week	Session 1 (Tuesday)	Session 2 (Thursday)
1	Dribbling	Open
2	Passing	Open
3	Receiving	Open
4	Shooting	Open
5	Heading	Open
6	Dribbling	Open
7	Passing	Open
8	Shooting	Open

Think of each phase as a season within itself. For each mini-season, you could preassign a topic for every training session, or you could use the plan-one-session/leave-one-session-open approach.

One of the advantages of planning the season in phases is the obvious flexibility it affords to your coaching. Rather than having to revise season-long plans if things do not go as expected (and they will not!), you have already taken that into account. This approach, however, will take more work and will require more thought.

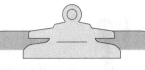

Coaching Tip

Use free play as a source of motivation for players. Keep players on task during a learning exercise by reminding them that they will get to play after they are done, or that if they do not work hard or stay on task they will not play.

Most younger players need work on all aspects of the game, making the full-season plan appropriate. As players become older and more experienced, you will find that their needs will change, and because of different rates of learning between individuals, you may find the phase-planning approach to work better for your needs. Regardless of the process you choose, have some idea of what you would like to accomplish by the end of the season.

SAMPLE TRAINING PLANS

The appendix provides a few training plans that contain all the necessary ingredients for a successful session. Each plan has a theme, and includes a warm-up, main activity, and final game phase. In addition, each training session comprises activities that are developmentally appropriate for the age groups being coached and is presented on a sample practice planning form.

SUMMARY

When working with your team, it is important to plan ahead. You should not only plan your practice sessions, but also your long-term approach to the season. Keep organizational ideas in mind when planning, and try to develop training sessions that end with a game. Coaches who practice a player-development philosophy realize that individual improvement and development are their measures of success. These coaches plan their seasons and practices accordingly.

7

THE EIGHT TECHNIQUES REQUIRED FOR SUCCESS

TECHNIQUE IS THE FOUNDATION of soccer. Of the four components of the game—technique, tactics, physical fitness, and psychology—none is more important than technique. Because the technical ability of your players will determine how well your team plays, it should be your highest priority.

During a game, your team will always be in one of two situations—either they will have the ball or they won't. Possession of the ball is necessary to score (unless opponents score upon themselves). A team may have attacking tactics that are superior to the opposition, but unless the team is in possession of the ball, the tactics are of no use. A team might be in better condition than the other team, but unless they can keep the ball, the best to hope for is a scoreless tie. You may be able to motivate and influence the psychological aspects of your players, but unless they possess the ball, they will likely be defeated more often than they win.

This does not mean you should have a win-at-all-costs mentality or a philosophy that success depends on victories. This simply means that technical development is the most important area for attention. If you use economical activities that allow players to practice more than one component of soccer at a time, then you will improve tactics, fitness, and the mental aspect of the game while working on technique.

Girls and boys carry out all techniques the same way. The only difference may occur with older players and is in the outcome, rather than the execution, of the technique. Because of their greater muscle mass, males usually can kick balls further and with more speed than can females. However, the techniques are performed in the same manner. Therefore you should coach the player, not the gender. Strive to teach the correct way to perform the techniques of the game, and you will develop championship athletes—male or female.

All soccer techniques have one thing in common—the ball. Some techniques, such as juggling, dribbling, and ball control, focus on the individual player keeping possession of the ball. Some, such as passing, shooting, and heading, concentrate on the individual player getting the ball to another person or place. Tackling, heading, and goalkeeping center on getting the ball away from the other team.

This chapter contains eight sections, each explaining a different technique. Examples of when and why a player would use the technique are presented. Each section ends with a table describing common problems and their possible causes and solutions.

JUGGLING

Juggling is the ability to keep the ball in the air repeatedly using various body parts. Players may juggle during a match, but it is really a training exercise. A player might use her feet, thighs, chest, head, or shoulders. Beginning players will tend to focus on using their thighs, probably because the thigh offers the greatest surface area and makes ball control easier. Encourage your players to experiment with using different body parts.

Players juggle to improve their *touch,* or the ability to make the ball do what they want, as well as their agility and understanding of how the ball reacts when struck with different body parts. By mastering juggling, players will become more proficient at controlling the ball, so it is a tremendous confidence booster. Juggling is easy to practice individually, it challenges the players, and it is a great source of "homework" that players can practice before and after training. The best jugglers are not necessarily the best soccer players; however, a player who is adept at juggling will usually have a greater proficiency with other techniques.

Following are descriptions of various juggling exercises. Each exercise focuses on a different body part. With each juggling exercise, allow the ball to drop toward the chosen body part.

STEPS TO SUCCESS: JUGGLING WITH THE FEET

1. Let the ball drop below the waist.
2. Lock the ankle and point the toe away from the body with the shoelaces facing the sky (upward).
3. The kicking leg should be slightly bent, and the action should come from the hip.
4. Use the shoelaces to contact the ball.
5. Play the ball with little or no spin.

STEPS TO SUCCESS: JUGGLING WITH THE THIGH

1. Raise the leg with the knee bent at a right angle. The thigh should be parallel with the ground.
2. Spread the arms away from the body for balance.
3. Contact the ball with the soft area on the front of the thigh (the muscle), not the hard area (the knee).

STEPS TO SUCCESS: JUGGLING WITH THE HEAD

1. Direct the forehead upward. Tilt the head back and look toward the sky.

FIGURE 7.1
Juggling with the feet

FIGURE 7.2
Juggling with the thigh

FIGURE 7.3
Juggling with the head

Table 7.1   Correcting Juggling Problems

Problem	Possible Causes and Solutions
Ball has no power (does not rise off of the foot).	Encourage player to lock the ankle. Have the player extend her ankle so her toe is pointed away. Try to move her ankle with your hand. The ankle should remain firm.
Ball flies away from the player.	The player is leaning backward. Encourage the player to stay over the ball. Players tend to reach for the ball with their foot, resulting in the ball flying away.
Ball is going too high.	Encourage the player to relax and to focus on striking the ball a certain height in the air.
When using the head, the ball does not move very high.	Bend and straighten the legs to increase power.

2. Use the toes and knees to generate the upward movement of the body. The head and neck should remain steady.

3. Lift upward through the center of the ball. Keep the eyes on the ball.

4. Adjust the body to prepare for the next juggle.

Pickups

To start juggling, players start the ball from the ground using a *pickup,* which is usually executed without the hands. Encourage your players to experiment with different types of pickups. Four basic methods include the front jump, reverse jump, roll and flick, and penguin. The object is to lift the ball off the ground and begin juggling before the ball bounces. However, players should feel free, especially when first learning, to allow the ball to bounce before juggling. When teaching a pickup to a beginning team, have play-

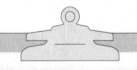

Coaching Tip

Allow players to experiment with different ways to get the ball off the ground. Challenge your players to develop new and different ways that they can show to their teammates when practicing.

ers catch the ball with their hands from the pickup while perfecting the action. Although it is fine to let younger players start the ball with their hands, as they become older and more experienced, they should be encouraged to start the ball from the ground.

STEPS TO SUCCESS: THE FRONT JUMP PICKUP

1. Squeeze the ball between the ankles.
2. Jump, and while in the air, lift the knees toward the chest and release the ball in front of the body.
3. Toss the ball high enough so there is enough time to land and be in a position to juggle.

STEPS TO SUCCESS: THE REVERSE JUMP PICKUP

1. Begin with the ball squeezed between the ankles.
2. When jumping, kick the feet behind by bending the knees. Keep the thighs straight.
3. Release the ball behind the back, and twist while in the air to face the ball.

FIGURE 7.4
The front jump pickup

FIGURE 7.5
The reverse jump pickup

STEPS TO SUCCESS: THE ROLL AND FLICK PICKUP

1. Place the sole of a foot on the ball.
2. The ball should be as far away from the body as possible so that the leg is nearly straight.
3. Roll the ball backward toward the body by bending at the knee.
4. Let the ball roll up the shoelaces of the performing foot. (Use the foot like a ramp.)
5. Flick the foot forward by straightening at the knee to lift the ball into the air.

STEPS TO SUCCESS: THE PENGUIN PICKUP

1. Stand behind the ball with the feet on either side of it, so the heels are close to each other but the toes are far away. (Think of making a V with the feet.)
2. The insides of both feet should be barely touching the ball and the knees should be slightly bent. Players look like penguins—hence the name.
3. Center the weight on both heels, and snap the feet together underneath the ball. The motion of the feet beneath the ball will propel it upward. The heels stay in contact with the ground at all times.
4. After the feet come together, scoot back about half a foot or so. Otherwise, the ball may hit the shins or knees.

FIGURE 7.6
The roll and flick pickup

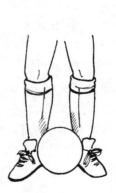

FIGURE 7.7
The penguin pickup

Table 7.2   Correcting Pickup Problems

Problem	Possible Causes and Solutions
The ball gets stuck between the legs (front or reverse jump).	At the height of the jump, spread the ankles slightly to release the ball.
The ball remains on the ground (front or reverse jump).	Place the ball firmly between the ankles.
The ball does not go very high (front or reverse jump).	The height of the ball is dependent upon the jump. The player should jump as high as possible. Use the feet like hands to toss the ball upward.
The ball doesn't roll high enough on the shoelaces (roll and flick).	Move the foot backward fast enough to give the ball momentum, but not so fast as to lose control.
The ball goes away from the player (roll and flick).	Flick quickly and contact underneath the ball.
The ball does not leave the feet or go very high (penguin).	Clap the feet together faster. The faster the feet move underneath the ball, the higher it will go.
The ball flies away or to one side of the player (penguin).	Stand close to the ball, and move both feet equally.

JUGGLING CHALLENGES

Work on juggling during the warm-up and skills phase of your training sessions. Always issue a goal or challenge to help keep players on task. Make challenges as individually based as possible. Focus on correct technique and individual achievement. Allow beginners to start the ball with their hands, but encourage the use of pickups as much as possible.

Juggling with a Bounce (U8 appropriate)

Players juggle, but a bounce is allowed between each touch. Start the ball from the hands, and work on correct repetitions.

Juggling Challenges (U8 and older)

Challenges might be addressed to the team (Who can juggle the ball 25 times?) or to individuals (Who can break their personal record?). Challenges might be based on using certain body parts. This approach is a great motivator for extra work.

DRIBBLING

Players dribble when they move with the ball. Of all the soccer techniques, *dribbling* is the most important. Mastering the various types of dribbling allows individuals to maintain possession of the ball. Players often have to cover a lot of space very quickly with the ball. They also have to be able to beat defenders using dribbling moves and fakes. They need to be able to change direction and move away from pressure while maintaining possession. This requires agility and the knowledge of dribbling maneuvers. When pressured by an opponent, the players must also know how to protect or shield the ball.

Many players earn their reputations from their mastery of dribbling. One of the most delightful actions to watch during a soccer game is a player faking and beating an opponent. Players learn their favorite fakes through trial and error, and usually become so

Coaching Tip
Dribbling feints often take years to perfect. Players who can complete a move in practice might be reluctant to do the same in a game because they fear failing. Recognize attempts to execute a move, even if the result was unsuccessful.

Personal Record
Each player establishes a personal juggling record. Every successful juggle earns a point. See how many points each player can earn before the ball hits the ground or the player loses the ball.

Juggling Boxes
Attempt to juggle in the following order: right foot, right thigh, left thigh, left foot, right foot. One complete circuit forms a box. Who can complete the most boxes?

Juggling the Empire State Building
Similar to juggling boxes, but with the head added (right foot, right thigh, head, left thigh, left foot, and right foot).

Partner Juggle (U10 and older)
Juggle with partners. Each person may touch the ball no more than twice in a row, and the ball may bounce between the partners. Who can juggle the most times? You could also award a letter for each successful juggle and see which pair can spell a word first, such as your team name, state, or any word that is appropriate. This is one way to take a simple task and disguise it as a new and different exercise.

good at one or two that they can beat all defenders—even those who know what to expect. The moves that the players choose reflect their creativity. New fakes are being developed all the time—that is the beauty of the game!

Speed Dribbling

Speed dribbling is used when a player is dribbling in an open space. The object is to move as quickly as possible while maintaining possession of the ball.

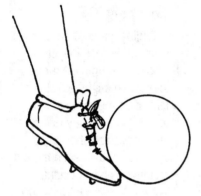

FIGURE 7.8
Foot-to-ball contact point when speed dribbling

STEPS TO SUCCESS: SPEED DRIBBLING

1. Use a long stride to push the ball forward.
2. The toe should be down, and the ball should be touched without breaking stride.
3. Contact the ball with the top part of the shoe between the toe and shoelaces (see figure 7.8).
4. Push the ball ahead far enough to be able to run at top speed for a few steps without the ball, but not so far that an opponent might steal it.

Dribbling to Beat Defenders

There are many types of dribbling fakes used to beat opponents. Every fake involves a change in speed, a change in direction, or a combination of the two. When beating an opponent, the object is to

Table 7.3 Correcting Problems with Speed Dribbling	
Problem	**Possible Causes and Solutions**
The ball goes too far away from the player.	Encourage the player to push rather than kick the ball.
The player is not running as fast as she can.	Use the top part of the foot to push the ball. When the inside of her foot is used, the leg must turn, which slows the player down.

get into the space behind her. Dribbling fakes are designed to cause the opponent to move to one side, thus freeing the other side. Players change their speed or direction of dribble to force the defender to lose balance or to make an incorrect choice.

Most dribbling moves have two variations. The main fake is the actual move. However, there will be times when the opponent either does not fall for the fake or recovers quickly enough to make the move ineffective. Therefore players often develop a countermove to deal with this situation. A common move and its counter are the scissors and double scissors.

Coaching Tip
Many female players are uncomfortable with speed dribbling. Spend as much time working on this skill as you spend teaching dribbling feints.

The *scissors* move is used to open up the space to one side of a defender by faking to the opposite side. The move gets its name from the motion of the legs, which open and close like a pair of scissors. When performing the move, the player fakes with one leg and takes the ball with the other.

STEPS TO SUCCESS: SCISSORS

1. The ball should be near the foot that the player will use for the fake.
2. Imagine standing on a big clock, with 12 o'clock on the ground directly in front and 6 o'clock directly behind. The key locations on the clock are 1 o'clock and 11 o'clock, which represent the space that would be immediately to the left and right of the defender.
3. Dip the left shoulder to sell the fake. Step over or in front of the ball with the left foot to 11 o'clock. Do not touch the ball, but fake to take the ball.
4. Immediately take the ball with the outside of the right foot toward 1 o'clock.
5. Use the inside of the right foot to push the back toward 12 o'clock to get into the space behind the defender.
6. The move can and should be practiced with the opposite feet (that is, right foot fakes and left foot takes).

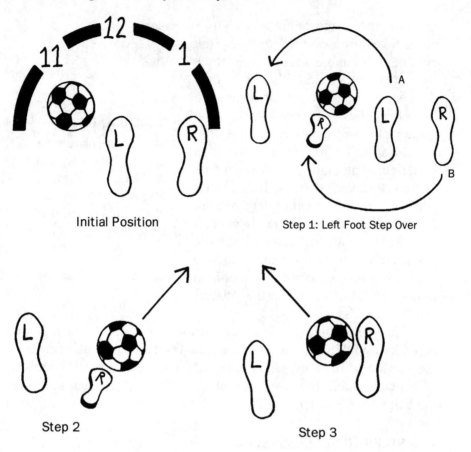

FIGURE 7.9
Moves involved in scissors

The *double scissors* is the countermove to the scissors. When performing the double scissors, instead of faking once, the player fakes twice.

STEPS TO SUCCESS: DOUBLE SCISSORS

1. Fake first with one foot, as in the scissors.
2. Then fake with the other in the exact same manner.
3. Take the ball with the outside of the initial foot.
4. Cut the ball back with the inside of the initial foot into the space behind the defender.

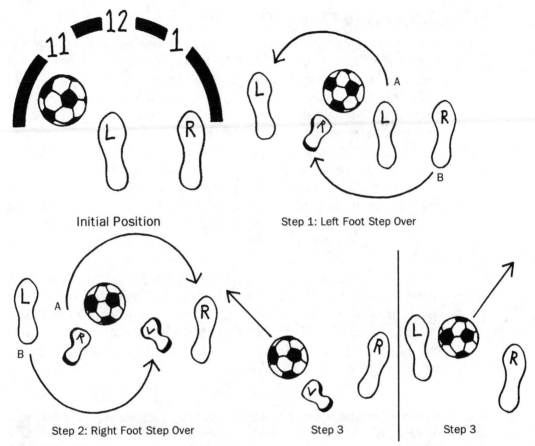

Initial Position

Step 1: Left Foot Step Over

Step 2: Right Foot Step Over

Step 3

Step 3

FIGURE 7.10
Moves involved in double scissors

Table 7.4 Correcting Problems with Scissors	
Problem	**Possible Causes and Solutions**
The ball goes too far away from the player.	Encourage the player to push rather than kick the ball.
The defender does not fall for the fake.	Have the ball carrier lunge, or "sell" the fake. Encourage use of the shoulders and arms to enhance the feint.
The ball carrier does not get past the defender, even though the fake works.	Make sure that the ball is being pushed past the defender (toward 1 or 11 o'clock). Because the outside of the foot is used to take the ball, many players push the ball sideways, instead of past the defender.

Dribbling to Change Direction

Players change direction to dribble away from an area. Perhaps the player is dribbling toward a sideline or corner and must change direction before she goes out of bounds. Or maybe the player is dribbling into an area in which there are many defenders, and she feels that it would be safer to change direction because there is not enough space available to dribble past the opponents. Changes of direction can be used to put defenders off balance, which will allow them to be beaten.

No matter what method is used to change direction, the ball carrier must be in control of her body. She must be able to stop and start while keeping possession of the ball, which requires agility. Two common ways that players change direction are cutting and turning the ball.

A player *cuts the ball* by changing the ball's roll by a sharp angle. Players should work on cutting the ball with the outside and inside of both feet. The ball should roll in front of a player after it is cut with the insides of the feet. Players using the outside of their feet cut the ball to roll it behind them. The technique used is similar no matter which part of the foot used.

Table 7.5 Correcting Cutting and Turning Problems	
Problem	**Possible Causes and Solutions**
When cutting the ball, the ball rolls toward the defender.	Contact the front half of the ball for a sharper cut.
The defender is not fooled by the cut.	The cut needs to be explosive. The player can also fake a pass with the foot used to cut the ball by raising the arms and accentuating a back swing of the leg just prior to cutting the ball.
The defenders are able to stay with the dribbler after the turn.	Accelerate with the touch occurring immediately after the turn.
When turning, the ball rolls too far behind the player.	Roll the ball and turn in the same motion. Many times players will first roll the ball, and then turn. By that time the ball is too far away.

FIGURE 7.11
Cutting the ball

STEPS TO SUCCESS: CUTTING THE BALL

1. Slow down to prepare for the change in direction.
2. If the ball is on the right foot, use the inside of the right foot to cut the ball to the left.
3. Have the ankle extended, and reach to contact the ball on the front outside.
4. The ball should sharply roll in front of and across the body to the left foot.
5. Immediately take the ball with the outside of the left foot.

Players *turn the ball* to completely change direction (a 180-degree turn).

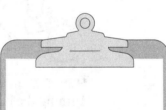

Coaching Tip
Female players tend to use cuts more than any other move to put defenders off balance.

STEPS TO SUCCESS: TURNING THE BALL

1. Stop the body and lean slightly back.
2. Place the sole of the foot on the ball and roll the ball behind the body.
3. In the same motion of the roll, turn to face the opposite direction.
4. Turn in the same direction of the foot used to roll the ball. If the left foot is used, turn to the left.
5. The ball should remain within playing distance at all times.

FIGURE 7.12
Turning the ball

Shielding

When *shielding*, the player places her body between the ball and the defender to keep the defender from getting to the ball. As long as the player can touch the ball, shielding is legal (a player blocking a defender without being in control of the ball is guilty of obstruction). Players shield the ball to maintain possession while also maintaining space. If a player dribbles backward, she might keep the ball, but she has lost valuable space on the field.

Shielding will only occur for a few seconds. The defender will not stay in the same position, but will instead try to run around the ball carrier to steal the ball. When the defender makes her move, the ball carrier should turn to the opposite side to take the ball past the defender.

STEPS TO SUCCESS: SHIELDING

1. Stand side-on (sideways) between the ball and the defender.
2. Make the body as big as possible by spreading the legs as far as possible while maintaining balance.
3. Use the entire body to block the defender.
4. The ball should be near the outside of the foot furthest from the defender.
5. The shoulder and forearm should hold off the defender.

FIGURE 7.13
Shielding

Table 7.6 Correcting Problems with Shielding

Problem	Possible Causes and Solutions
The player is moving backward.	The player is not absorbing pressure, but is moving away from the pressure. Encourage the player to lean into the defender and to consistently adjust her feet to maintain balance.
The defender can reach the ball by extending her leg.	The player is not making her body big enough. Stand side-on to place the ball as far from the defender as possible.

PASSING

Players pass the ball to maintain possession and to set up scoring opportunities. Players can pass with the inside, instep, and outside of their feet. They might also try to play balls on the ground, balls in the air, or balls that curve. Two people—the passer and the receiver—are necessary for a successful pass. Teach your players about the importance of executing the pass correctly and the need for a teammate to receive the ball. Make sure that players are using both feet. Players frequently use only their preferred foot, but success later in their soccer career will be easier to attain if they can use both feet equally.

The Inside-of-the-Foot Pass

The *inside-of-the-foot pass* (push pass) is the most basic pass and is used when playing the ball over a short distance. It is the easiest type

DRIBBLING GAMES AND EXERCISES

Red Light, Green Light (U8 appropriate)

Each player has a ball at the starting line. The traffic cop (coach or player) stands on the finishing line 10–15 yards away. On "Green light," the players may dribble. When "Red light" is called, the players' balls must be stopped. Any player who has a ball that is still moving must return to the starting line. The winner, or winners, are those who can dribble past the finishing line. *Note:* The requirement that the ball must be stopped forces the players to keep the ball near them at all times.

Dribbling Through Gates

In the playing area, randomly set out multiple 1- to 2-yard-wide gates (goals). The playing area should be appropriate for the number of players. Set up as many goals as possible. Players may score by dribbling through any goal in any direction.

Variation 1 (U8 appropriate): Each player has a ball. Who can score the most goals in one minute? Allow players to score on the same goal multiple times, or restrict the players to score on a different goal each time.

Variation 2 (U10 and older): Multiple groups play 1 V 1. Whoever has the ball can score, the other defends. All partner groups can play at the same time. Who can score the most goals in one minute? Play successive rounds, and change partners.

of pass to play accurately, because there is a large surface contacting the ball. In general, inside-of-the-foot passes are played on the ground.

STEPS TO SUCCESS: INSIDE-OF-THE-FOOT PASS

1. Approach the ball on a slight angle.
2. Place the plant foot (supporting leg's foot) next to the ball, with the toe pointed at the target.
3. Use a compact back swing that is long enough to generate enough power for the pass.
4. Aim the inside of the foot at the target. Lock the ankle, with the toe up and heel down.
5. Keep the eyes on the ball and strike at its center with the inside of the kicking foot.
6. Follow through toward the target.

Variation 3 (U10 and older): Break group into two teams. Use half as many balls as players (for two teams of five, use five balls). Which team can score the most goals in one minute? Players can score or shield to maintain possession. Any player can defend any other player, which introduces double-teaming.

Gauntlet

Break the squad into two teams. Make a column of three or four 10-yard-by-10-yard grids. One team defends and the other attacks. The defending team has a defender in each grid. The attacking team tries to dribble through the gauntlet. Each defender must stay in her own grid. Rotate defenders at a time interval or after they successfully knock the ball away from an attacker. Attackers score a point by successfully dribbling through the gauntlet. Which team can score the most goals in five minutes?

Variation 1 (U8 appropriate): Place defenders in every other grid, forming a safe area between grids. Defenders are Sharks, attackers are Minnows. Who can swim (dribble their ball under control) to the other side?

Variation 2 (U10 and older): Allow multiple attackers to go at the same time. This encourages tactical planning by the attacking team. Place a regulation goal for players to shoot into.

Variation 3 (U10 and older): Attackers can only dribble forward, which requires them to take on and beat defenders while making quick decisions.

FIGURE 7.14
The inside-of-the-foot pass

Table 7.7 Correcting Problems with the Inside-of-the-Foot Pass	
Problem	**Possible Causes and Solutions**
The pass is not accurate.	Follow through directly toward the target. The inside of the passing foot should be perpendicular to the direction of the intended pass.
The ball does not stay on the ground.	The player contacted the bottom of the ball or did not follow through. Use a fluid passing motion that does not stop at ball contact.
The pace of the pass is too soft.	Strike the ball harder. An approach of two or three steps prior to passing will help provide momentum for the passing leg.

The Driven Pass

Players use a *driven pass* to play the ball over longer distances. Players might drive the ball on the ground or in the air. Usually players use a driven ball when playing a pass over a distance longer than they are able to with an inside-of-the-foot pass, or when they must get the ball to their target quickly. The general technique for passes in the air is the same used for passes on the ground. The difference between the passing motions mainly lies in the location of the supporting foot and the lean of the body at contact. When passing a driven ball, players use their insteps, or shoelaces.

STEPS TO SUCCESS: THE DRIVEN PASS

1. Use an angled two- or three-step approach.
2. The last step prior to planting the supporting foot should be slightly longer to help generate more power.
3. Plant the supporting foot next to the ball for a ground pass, or slightly behind the ball for an air pass. The foot should be close enough to the ball to allow contact, but not so close to cause difficulty following through.
4. The plant-foot toe should be aimed at the target. The toe of the kicking foot should be pointed and the ankle locked to provide a firm and large passing surface.
5. Strike the center of the ball for a ground pass or slightly below the center for an air pass. The head should be down, and the eyes should be on the ball.
6. For an air pass, lean back slightly. For a pass along the ground, lean over the ball. In both cases, also lean to the side away from the ball (leaning to the left if passing with the right foot).
7. Use the arms to help maintain balance by bringing the opposite arm across the body during the kicking motion.
8. The follow-through should be long and should come slightly across the body. The higher the pass, the higher the passing foot should come off of the ground.

FIGURE 7.15
Driven pass at contact

Table 7.8 Correcting Problems with the Driven Pass

Problem	Possible Causes and Solutions
The pass is not accurate.	The follow-through was not directly at the target. The kicking leg should swing directly at the target and across the body after contacting the ball.
The player miscontacted the ball.	The ball should be struck along its centerline.
The pass is too slow.	The player did not hit the ball hard enough. Encourage a strong leg swing. Prepare the ball by pushing it at a slight angle so the leg can straighten but the toe does not contact the ground.
The ball goes too high.	The player was leaning back as she struck the ball, or her support foot was too far behind the ball. Lean over the ball as it is struck.
The ball stays on the ground when the player is trying to pass the ball in the air.	The player contacted the ball on its upper half, or she had her support too far forward. Lean back when striking the ball, and have a long follow-through.

The Outside-of-the-Foot Pass

The *outside-of-the-foot pass* is used to disguise passes. Players use the outside of the foot to pass the ball while running with it, as they are better able to continue moving without changing their stride. This type of pass usually is effective over a short distance, because power is exchanged for surprise.

STEPS TO SUCCESS:
THE OUTSIDE-OF-THE-FOOT PASS

1. The ball should be close to the body, off to one side.
2. Use a small backswing involving bending at the knee.
3. Rotate the ankle inward slightly so the outside of the foot is aimed at the ball.
4. Strike the inside rear of the ball so it travels on an angle away from the body (see figure 7.16).

FIGURE 7.16
Outside-of-the-foot pass at contact

Table 7.9 Correcting Problems with the Outside-of-the-Foot Pass	
Problem	**Possible Causes and Solutions**
The pass is not accurate.	The foot was not oriented correctly. The ball will leave the foot in the direction that the outside of the foot is facing. Turn the foot inward just prior to passing the ball.
The pass is too soft.	The backswing did not provide sufficient power. Pass the ball while running, so the passing motion is a part of the stride.

5. Follow-through is short and compact, resembling the length of a running stride.

Curved Passes

Players can *curve the ball* by playing it with a sideways spin. The ball will curve in the direction that the front of the ball is spinning. If you were to look over the top of the ball, a clockwise spin would result in a ball flight that curves from left to right. A counter-clockwise spin curves the ball from right to left. The amount that the ball curves is directly related to how fast the ball is spinning. Curved passes usually travel in the air and are used during long passes or shots.

Soccer players try to curve balls for various reasons. They might be trying to pass the ball around an object, or they might know that a curved ball could be more difficult for the goalkeeper to save. Curved passes can be struck with the inside, outside, or instep (laces) of the foot. This type of pass requires enough strength to play the ball over a longer distance, so it is a skill that is appropriate to practice with players who are 10 years and older.

STEPS TO SUCCESS: CURVED PASSES WITH
THE INSIDE OF THE FOOT

1. Approach the ball on an angle.
2. Place the planting foot behind and to the side of the ball.
3. Lean back—the kicking foot should be moving upward when the ball is struck.
4. Strike with the inside of the foot across the back half of the ball off center.
5. Follow through away from the target to the outside.

FIGURE 7.17
Curving the ball

Table 7.10 Correcting Problems with the Curved Pass

Problem	Possible Causes and Solutions
The ball does not curve.	There was not enough spin on the ball. Strike the ball harder along its backside.
The ball goes too high.	The player was leaning too far back. The plant foot should be next to the ball, and the player should lean back slightly when striking the ball.
The pass is not accurate.	The player struck the side of the ball. Contact the back of the ball and follow through to the outside.

An Important Passing Issue

When working on passing, keep in mind that players need to experience for themselves the best way to perform each method. While you should look for proper technique and be able to correct mistakes, allow players to learn on their own the different ways to pass the ball. Your concern should be more toward helping them learn the action and less about the actual way the skill was performed. The only requirement for success is that the ball gets from the passer to its intended target. Unless working on a specific type of pass, do not be concerned with the surface of the foot used, or about the leg swing or follow-through if the ball got to where it was supposed to go.

Coaching Tip

Try to use the term "ball control" instead of "trap." Players should not "capture" and stop the ball. Instead they should control it and keep it moving.

BALL CONTROL

Just as the passer executes a pass, the receiver must *control the incoming ball.* Players use various parts of their bodies to control incoming balls, whether coming from a teammate or intercepted from the opponents. A mastery of ball control increases a player's ability to maintain possession.

Ball Control on the Ground

A majority of passes, especially with younger players, are played along the ground. Players attempt to control any ball played to them along the ground unless choosing to pass immediately, which is known as a one-touch pass. Controlling the ball requires that the player have space available to control the ball and is aware of where that space is located. It could be to the right, left, in front, or behind. Sometimes a player may be completely open, but at least one, if not more, of the areas nearby may contain some source of pressure. The inside or outside of the receiving foot is used when controlling the ball on the ground.

STEPS TO SUCCESS: RECEIVING BALLS ON THE GROUND

1. Move into the path of the ball.
2. Expose the chosen surface (inside or outside of the foot) to the ball. Bend the knee of the receiving leg, and balance the body's weight on the supporting leg.
3. Take the speed off of the ball at contact by slightly moving the foot backward.
4. Redirect the ball slightly away and to one side of the body so that the next touch could be a pass if necessary. Push it into an open space as far away from any defenders as possible to allow time to decide the next action.

PASSING GAMES AND EXERCISES

Marbles (U8 appropriate)

Each player has a ball. Play begins with each ball being kicked at the same time. One player passes her ball some distance away. The other player attempts to hit her partner's ball with her own ball. Alternate passes until the balls make contact. The player who passes the ball into her partner's receives a point, and restarts play by passing her ball away. Play to a predetermined score or for a certain time limit. Extra points could be awarded for different types of passes (laces, outside of the foot, using the opposite foot).

Passing through Gates (U8 and U10 appropriate)

Use cones or markers to set up various 2-yard-wide gates randomly in a 20-yard-by-20-yard playing area. Break the team into groups of partners with a ball. Which group can complete the most passes through the gates in a given time? All groups play at the same time. Any passes touching a cone or not received cleanly do not count.

Variation 1: No restrictions. Who can score the most points?

Variation 2: A team may not score through one gate more than twice in a row.

Variation 3: Players must use a certain type of pass or a certain foot for the point to count, or they could receive bonus points for a certain type of pass.

4 V 2 (U10 and U12 appropriate)

In a 15-yard-by-12-yard grid, four players try to keep the ball away from two defenders. Both defenders stay in the middle of the grid. The attackers stand

FIGURE 7.18
Receiving balls on the ground

on the grid borders and may move from side to side. They may not, however, leave the gridline. The defenders try to touch the ball. A defender who touches the ball changes places with one of the attacking players. If the attacking players can complete four passes, they earn a point. Have a competition between two groups to see who can score the most during a given time.

3-Team Possession (U12 appropriate)

Break the team into three groups. A team of 15 will have three groups of five. It is okay to have uneven teams if you have an uneven number of players. Each group should wear a different color bib. In a grid large enough to allow success, two groups try to keep the ball from one group. Play continues for a certain time.

Variation 1: The defending team stays the same for a given time. Rotate so all teams have a chance to defend. Count the number of passes completed by the two attacking groups. The team that completes the most passes during its two attacking rounds wins.

Variation 2: All teams defend for a given time, as in variation one. However, if the defending team wins the ball, they try to keep it from the other two groups. Score as in variation 1, but explain to the players that if the defending team can intercept the ball and keep possession, it decreases the number of passes that the other two teams will be able to complete.

Variation 3: When the defending team intercepts the ball, they try to dribble out of the grid. If they are successful, they change with the group who gave up the ball. Which group can be on attack the most?

Table 7.11 Correcting Problems with Receiving Balls on the Ground	
Problem	**Possible Causes and Solutions**
The ball comes to a complete stop.	The sole of the player's foot was used, or there was too much cushioning. Attempt to slow the ball, but not stop it completely. Make sure that the appropriate surface is used and the ankle is firm. Receive with a motion that redirects the ball away from the defender.
The ball bounces away from the player.	The foot moved toward the ball when making contact. Remain balanced and receive the ball with a cushioning motion.
The ball bounces into the air.	Contact was too low on the ball. Contact the ball slightly above the center half to keep the ball on the ground.
The player misses the ball.	The player did not get into the path of the ball. Anticipate the pass and move early to receive the ball.

Ball Control in the Air

Balls out of the air are controlled with the feet, thighs, or chest. The general rule of thumb for controlling the ball out of the air is the lower the body part used, the easier the technique is to execute. However, the higher the ball is controlled out of the air, the greater the chance that your team can do something productive with it. Controlling with the feet may be easier, but it also may allow the opposing team to intercept the ball because it is in the air longer.

Use the feet to control the ball if it is too far away to reach with the thigh or chest or if there are no defenders near enough to intercept. The ball should be received below the waist. Therefore the flight of the ball is an issue. Try not to lift the foot higher than the waist to control a ball. Raising the foot too high not only places the player off balance, but it also could result in a dangerous-play foul against their team. Use the thigh to control balls that are coming almost straight down. Use the chest to control driven balls or balls that are traveling too high for the thigh or foot.

The chest control can be intimidating for girls, especially those who have entered puberty. Females, however, must learn to perform this skill. They must master the chest trap to develop as a player for the future. Frequent practice will help players to develop the confidence necessary to control the ball with their chests.

STEPS TO SUCCESS: RECEIVING WITH THE FEET

1. Get in the path of the ball.
2. While balancing on the standing leg, lift the receiving foot to contact the ball. The inside, outside, or instep may be used, depending on the path of the ball.
3. Spread the arms away from the body for balance.
4. Take power away from the ball at contact. The motion is the opposite of juggling. The ball should come off of the foot with a slight bounce, no more than a few inches from the foot.
5. Immediately dribble away with the ball.

STEPS TO SUCCESS: RECEIVING WITH THE THIGH

1. Get in the path of the ball.
2. While balancing on the standing leg, lift the receiving thigh parallel to the ground. Lift the thigh early enough to be in the correct position when the ball arrives, but not so early to cause a loss of balance.

FIGURE 7.19
Receiving with the feet

FIGURE 7.20
Receiving with the thigh

3. Spread the arms away from the body for balance.
4. Receive the ball with the muscular part of the front of the thigh (not the knee). Give with the thigh slightly to take power away from the ball.
5. The ball should come off of the thigh with a slight bounce, no more than a few inches from the thigh.
6. Contact the ball with the foot before it hits the ground to eliminate any bouncing.
7. Immediately dribble away with the ball.

FIGURE 7.21
Receiving with the chest

STEPS TO SUCCESS: RECEIVING WITH THE CHEST

1. Get in the path of the ball.
2. Have both feet in contact with the ground. Be on the balls of the feet with the knees slightly bent.
3. Spread the arms away from the body for balance and to increase the area available for the control. Make a table for the ball to land upon.
4. Receive the ball on the upper part of the chest, directly below the shoulder blades. Try not to receive the ball directly in the center of the chest because the breastbone sometimes causes the ball to bounce too far away.
5. The ball should rebound slightly in the air. Give at the waist and knees to take pace off of the ball.
6. Contact the ball with the foot before it hits the ground to eliminate any bouncing.
7. Immediately dribble away with the ball.

HEADING

Players use their heads to move the ball during attacking *and* defending situations. The forehead should always be used to head the ball. Heading the ball allows players to play the ball earlier than if they were to wait until the ball came to the ground. Although heading might be intimidating for your players, it is important that you teach

Table 7.12   Correcting Problems with Ball Control

Problem	Possible Causes and Solutions
The ball bounces away from the player and is too far away for her to maintain possession.	The player did not give when receiving the ball, regardless of the surface used. Cushion the ball slightly at contact.
The player misjudges the ball.	The player moved too early or too late to get in the path of the ball. Frequent repetitions over time will help improve judgment.
The ball bounces too high during the initial attempt to control it.	The player moved into the ball rather than slightly away with the controlling surface. Maintain balance when receiving the ball.

them this skill so that they can perform the technique safely and correctly.

Heading to Attack

Players head the ball when *attacking* in order to shoot on goal or to pass to another player. The pass may be directly to a teammate, or it might be into a space where the player can run. In both cases, the objective is to direct the ball downward. One of the most common errors when heading to score occurs when the ball flies over the goal. When coaching players how to head to attack, teach them to head the ball down.

Coaching Tip

Coach your players to look directly at the target when heading the ball. When heading to score, teach them to look at the goal line.

STEPS TO SUCCESS: HEADING TO ATTACK

1. Lean back by flexing the knees and the waist.
2. As the player heads the ball, her forward motion should occur as a powerful bending forward at the hips (like a rubber band snapping into the ball). The neck and head should remain steady. Attack the ball.

BALL CONTROL GAMES AND EXERCISES

Star Wars (U8 appropriate)

All players have a ball within a 15-yard-by-15-yard grid. One player or coach is Darth Vader. Darth Vader's job is to try to tag the rest of the players. Two players or coaches stand outside of the grid without a ball. Any player that gets tagged must go to one of the outside players and pass the ball to her. The ball is tossed back to the player in the air. The receiving player must control the ball before dribbling away. Who can avoid being tagged?

Magic Square (U10 and older)

Half of the team is inside a 20-yard-by-20-yard grid with a ball. The rest of the players are spread out along the outside of the grid. The players dribble their balls and then pass to any players on the outside. The ball is returned to the passer, either in the air or on the ground. If the players along the outside of the grid are not able to accurately pass the ball in the air, allow them to pick up and toss the ball with their hands. Who can receive the most balls cleanly in a given amount of time?

3-Zone Game (U10 & Older)

Divide a rectangular grid into three zones. Break the team into three equal-sized groups. One group plays in each zone. The groups in each end zone are attacking while the group in the middle defends. Each team must stay within its area. The attacking groups attempt to pass the ball to each other or to the other attacking group, while the defending group works to intercept the ball. If the defenders steal the ball, they switch with the team that gave up the ball, and play continues. A defending team has a point scored against them if a pass is successfully played from one end to the other. The first team to have 3 points scored against them loses.

Variation 1: Everyone must stay in her own zone, but the attacking teams must complete at least three passes within their own zone before they can pass to the other side.

Variation 2: The defending team can send one player into the attacking zone to steal the ball. When the ball is passed to the other end, the defender must return to the middle zone, as shown in figure 7.22.

Variation 3: Attackers may not touch the ball more than twice when passing.

Note: Adjust the size of the playing area to foster success and to encourage a specific type of pass. If the central area is large, attacking players will have to pass in the air or with their insteps. A smaller central zone might allow inside-of-the-foot passes.

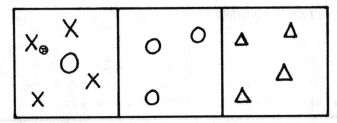

FIGURE 7.22
Variation on 3-zone game

FIGURE 7.23
Heading to attack

3. Contact the upper half of the ball with the forehead near the hairline.
4. Look at the target and follow through downward. Head the ball down.

Heading to Defend

Although the technique used when heading for defensive purposes is very similar to heading to attack, the objective is quite different. Heading to attack is used to get the ball to a specific target, whether goal, teammate, or space on the pitch. *Defensive heading* is used to get the ball away from the other team. Players attempt to head the ball high in the air and far away to stop the opponent's attack. Defensive heading usually occurs in front of the goal or when the opposition attempts a long pass over the fullbacks.

Table 7.13	Correcting Problems with Heading to Attack
Problem	**Possible Causes and Solutions**
The ball flies over the target.	The ball was contacted too early or the follow-through was upward. Look at the ground near the target while heading. When heading on goal, look at the goal line.
The ball goes straight up in the air.	The ball was played with the top of the head. Move the upper body to allow the forehead to contact the ball.
The ball has little power.	The player did not attack the ball, but rather let the ball hit her. Use the back and legs to provide power.

STEPS TO SUCCESS: HEADING TO DEFEND

1. Lean back by flexing the knees and the waist.
2. Keep the neck firm, and contact the ball with the forehead.
3. The forward motion should occur as a powerful bending forward at the hips. The neck and head should remain steady.
4. Head the lower half of the ball upward and away. A ball that goes upward but not far is better than a ball that goes down and far.
5. The head should be directed upward throughout the entire motion.

FIGURE 7.24
Heading to defend

Table 7.14   Correcting Problems with Heading to Defend

Problem	Possible Causes and Solutions
The ball does not go far enough away.	The player did not provide enough power. Explode through the ball. The power comes from the legs and back. Time any jumping headers to contact the ball at the height of the jump.
The ball flies too low.	The follow-through was too downward. Move through the ball and make contact while still slightly leaning back.

HEADING GAMES AND EXERCISES

Head It/Catch It (U8 appropriate)

Players form a circle around the coach, who has a ball in his or her hands. Use a foam ball if more appropriate. As you toss the ball to each player, call "Head it" or "Catch it." If heads are called, the player should catch the ball. If catch is called, the player should head the ball back to the coach. Who can go the longest without making a mistake?

2 V 2 Heading (U10 and older)

Players go two against two in an 8-yard-by-10-yard grid. They should play with the head and hands. One team defends one 8-yard endline, the other defends the opposite endline. The attacking players try to head the ball over the defenders' goal line at waist level or below. The defending team must remain on their goal line. The attacking team starts with the ball in their hands. One attacker tosses the ball to her teammate, who attempts to shoot or pass. Once the initial toss is completed, the attacking team may only use their heads. If the ball hits the ground or leaves the grid, the defending team takes over. Who can score the most goals?

Variation 1: The tosser can move in front of the defender's goal so she can toss the ball back toward the header.

Variation 2: The tosser must play the ball from the spot where it was turned over. After a goal, play begins from their goal line.

Variation 3: Diving header goals are worth extra points.

Toss-Head-Catch (U12 and older appropriate)

Two teams play against each other. The ball starts in one player's hands. The player with the ball tosses the ball to a teammate, who must head the ball. After the ball has been headed, another player may catch it. Players may head the ball to pass or to score on a goal. Players may not catch a tossed ball. They may only catch or intercept a headed ball. If the ball hits the ground, the defending team takes possession. Play on a field that would also be appropriate if the players were playing a regular game. Who can score the most goals?

FINISHING

Shooting is often referred to as *finishing.* Players finish in order to score goals. The technique of finishing differs slightly from passing in that there is no concern about a receiver being able to control the ball. However, finishing can be thought of more accurately as passing into the goal past the goalkeeper. Players usually finish in two different situations. (1) When players are far from the goal, a finish that has a lot of speed and distance, or power, is necessary. This is called *long-range finishing*. Use the instep when finishing with power. (2) When near to the goal, power is not necessary, but rather accuracy, or finesse, is more important. Players should become proficient at not only knowing how to perform each type of finish, but also when each type should be used.

Coaching Tip

As females grow older, they do not develop as much muscle mass as males do. This results in many older females being unable to strike balls with much power. When working with females, stress power *and* accuracy, rather than one over the other.

STEPS TO SUCCESS: LONG-RANGE FINISHING

1. Move quickly toward the ball on an angle to provide momentum.
2. The last step toward the ball should be as long as possible.
3. Plant the support foot next to the ball with the toe pointing toward the target.
4. With the eyes on the ball, strike its center with the instep. Make sure that the ankle is locked.
5. Follow through toward the goal.
6. After striking, land on the foot that kicked the ball.

Many times players will find themselves very close to the goal with the ball. This could occur after a pass or cross from a teammate, or during a breakaway. In

FIGURE 7.25
Long-range finishing

Table 7.15   Correcting Problems with Finishing

Problem	Possible Causes and Solutions
The finish is too weak.	The ankle was loose or the approach was too slow. Speed up or maintain speed prior to shooting.
The finish is not on target.	The follow-through was away from the goal, or the center of the ball was not struck. Keep the eyes on the ball when making contact and follow through at the goal.
The player strikes the ball over the top of the goal.	The player was leaning back at contact or the bottom half of the ball was hit. Strike the upper half of the ball, and land on the finishing foot after shooting.

either case, accuracy is much more important than power. One of the most frustrating things in soccer is to watch a player strike the ball incorrectly, resulting in a finish that flies over the top or wide of the goal. With short-range, or *finesse*, finishing, the objective is to play the ball with more concern for accuracy than power. The inside of the foot is the best surface for increasing accuracy.

STEPS TO SUCCESS: SHORT-RANGE FINISHING

1. Approach the ball without decreasing speed.
2. Plant the support foot next to the ball.
3. Strike the center of the ball with the inside of the foot.
4. Run through the ball. After shooting, continue to move in the original direction.
5. Follow through toward the goal. Pass the ball where the keeper is not located. (There are no bonus points for power!)

FIGURE 7.26
Short-range (finesse) finishing

Table 7.16 Correcting Problems with Finishing	
Problem	**Possible Causes and Solutions**
The ball misses the goal.	The follow-through was away from the goal, or the inside of the foot was not aimed correctly. Move toward the goal as the ball is struck.
The ball is finished directly at the goalkeeper.	The player aimed at the goalkeeper or did not aim at all. Pick out a target prior to striking the ball. Corners of the net or a spot on the net serve as good targets.
The player chooses the wrong foot for the shot.	Players sometimes try not to use their weaker foot when passing or shooting. When moving from left to right, the right foot will usually be the best foot to use, and vice versa. Practice finishing balls that can only be played with one foot or the other to increase confidence using both feet.

FINISHING GAMES AND EXERCISES

Push & Finish (U8 and older)

Set up two goals 30 yards apart. Use cones if necessary. Players line up at one post on each goal, so each line is diagonal from the other. Use multiple areas if the lines are too long. One player from each line simultaneously pushes the ball forward and finishes on the opposite goal. After finishing, the player collects her ball and joins the opposite line. Any player who misses the goal must sprint to get her ball. Switch starting sides to practice with both feet. Goalkeepers may be used in one or both goals but are not necessary. The important aspect of this exercise is to allow players as many opportunities to finish as possible during the practice.

2 V 2 Finishing (U10 and older)

This game is very similar to the 2 V 2 heading game. Each playing area should be 8 yards wide and 30 yards long, divided into two halves (both halves 8 yards by 15 yards). Each team must stay in its own half. The team without the ball must retreat to their goal line, where they act as goalkeepers.

TACKLING

Tackling is the only technique used only while defending. Players tackle the ball to knock it away from an opponent. There are different types of tackles, including the poke tackle, block tackle, and slide tackle (some leagues do not allow slide tackling, and it is a foul to slide tackle from behind). No matter which type is used, the player must always contact the ball prior to touching the opponent or else a foul may be called.

A successful tackle ends when the opponent loses the ball. If the tackler wins the ball for herself, that is great. However, the mentality should be that the tackler is trying to help her *team* win the ball. Many times players try to tackle and win the ball, and they end up doing neither because they were too tentative. Teach your players that if they choose to tackle, the opponent who had the ball must not remain with it. In most cases, however, patience is a better tool, because most opponents will end up losing the ball without being tackled.

The team with the ball tries to score by shooting the ball past the goalkeepers at head level or below. The attackers may pass among each other to set up a finish. Who can score the most goals?

3 Team Tourney (U10 and older appropriate)

Play in an area 36 yards long and 44 yards wide. Two teams play against each other while one team rests. When a goal is scored, the team who was scored upon leaves the field, and the resting team plays. The small field should allow for a lot of finishes. Which team can score the most goals?

Variation 1: The scoring team can choose to remain or to leave the field. Remind players that they cannot score unless they are playing.

Variation 2: The resting players position themselves around the outside of the grid and act as windows. Windows may be used by either team as helpers. The team with the ball may pass the ball to a window player, who must return it to a player on the team that passed it to her.

Variation 3: Position window players on either side of each goal. A goal may only be scored by a finish that is played after a pass from a window.

Coaching Tip

One of the most frustrating things you will have to deal with is players who attempt to tackle at incorrect times or who tackle but fail to win the ball. These players are *stabbing* or *diving in*. Teach players patience when defending. Set up practice activities where tackling is not allowed.

The Poke Tackle

When using a *poke tackle*, the toe of the foot nearest the ball carrier is used to tap the ball away. Poke tackles are effective because they usually surprise the ball carrier. If a player tries to tackle, however, and misses the ball, she will usually be beaten because she will become temporarily off balance. Players should only try to tackle the ball when they are sure that they can win it.

STEPS TO SUCCESS: THE POKE TACKLE

1. Jockey (move backward with) the ball carrier while side-on (front foot close to the ball, and the back foot closer to the goal). Shuffle, and avoid crossing the feet.

2. Tackle when the ball is between the ball carrier's touches.

3. Reach the front foot to the ball with a stabbing motion, and knock the ball away with the toe. Be patient—touch, touch, *tackle*.

4. If the ball is missed, immediately recover and continue to defend.

The Block Tackle

A *block tackle* is much more powerful than a poke tackle. When performed correctly, the opponent's momentum is used against her. A successful block tackle usually results in the tackler obtaining the ball and the ball carrier falling over the ball. The tackler blocks the ball with the inside of her foot.

FIGURE 7.27
The poke tackle

FIGURE 7.28
The block tackle

STEPS TO SUCCESS: THE BLOCK TACKLE

1. Jockey the ball carrier. Always move a few steps along with the attacker before attempting to tackle.
2. Tackle just before the ball carrier touches the ball.
3. Step toward the ball with the front foot, and then tackle with the inside of the back foot.
4. Lean forward and over the ball, and move through the ball toward the opponent.
5. Continue to move through the ball after making contact.

Table 7.17 Correcting Problems with Tackling	
Problem	**Possible Causes and Solutions**
The player does not dispossess the player with the ball.	The tackle was timed incorrectly or was executed too softly. Players should learn to be patient. But when choosing to tackle, they should do so with a complete commitment to dispossess the opponent.
The player makes contact with the ball but does not gain possession.	The ball was not hit hard enough. Follow through into the ball, regardless of the type of tackle chosen.

GOALKEEPING

Goalkeepers need to work on special techniques that are specific to that position. However, they must practice the basic skills of soccer, too, because there are instances when they might not be able to use their hands. The goalkeeper fills two roles: she stops the other team's attack, and she starts her team's attack. Goalkeepers stop attacks by catching the ball. They start attacks by distributing the ball to a teammate. Both roles require knowledge of a variety of techniques.

When catching the ball, it will be coming from one of two places: the ground or the air. The techniques used for these two cases differ slightly. When distributing the ball, goalkeepers frequently

TACKLING GAMES AND EXERCISES

Partner Block Tackle (U10 appropriate)

This exercise reinforces the correct method of block tackling. Break the team into partner groups, each with a ball. Partners stand facing each other with the ball between them. Each player places her hands on her partner's shoulders, with one foot next to the ball. Each player should place the same foot (e.g., the right foot) next to the ball. Players move the other foot back and away from the ball. The foot next to the ball should support the player's body weight; the rear foot is the tackling foot. The players say, "Ready, set, go." On "Ready" and "Set," each player brings her rear foot in contact with

punt or throw the ball. Punts are for longer range, while throws are for shorter distances.

Catching Balls on the Ground

Goalkeepers use a scooping catch when playing balls along the ground. The goalkeeper may bend at the waist or go down on one knee when catching the ball. Regardless of the method chosen, it is vital to be behind the ball in case it is missed. Goalkeepers use the scoop technique to catch rolling balls.

STEPS TO SUCCESS: CATCHING BALLS ON THE GROUND

FIGURE 7.29
Catching a ball on the ground

1. Get between the ball and the goal as early as possible.
2. Move both hands to the ball with the palms up and the fingers pointed down. Keep the elbows close together.
3. Cup the hands and allow the ball to roll up the forearms.
4. After the ball is caught, stand up and cradle the ball in both arms (as if holding a watermelon). Keep the upper arms below and the forearms in front of the ball.
5. Move forward and away from the goal throughout the entire process to avoid a collision with an opposing player (and to potentially begin a counterattack).

the ball softly, and on "Go" each player brings her rear foot to the ball as hard as possible. Each player should contact the ball at the same time. The objective of the exercise is to help each player experience what a good block tackle feels like.

1 V 1 Defending (U10 and older appropriate)

Play one against one in a rectangular grid. The player with the ball scores by dribbling over the opponent's endline. If the defender dispossess the attacker, she may score. Coach defenders to tackle only at appropriate times. In soccer, a player who tackles but misses the ball is usually beaten, so patience is important.

Catching Balls in the Air

Balls that are shot in the air may approach the goalkeeper in two areas—below the waist or above the waist. Shots below the waist should be caught with the scoop technique, similar to catching balls on the ground. Balls above the waist should be caught with the fingertips. The goalkeeper should use both hands whenever possible.

STEPS TO SUCCESS: CATCHING BALLS IN THE AIR

1. Move between the ball and the goal.
2. The arms should be straight with the elbows slightly bent.
3. For balls below the waist, keep the palms facing up and the pinkie fingers close together. For balls above the waist, keep fingers up and thumbs close together.
4. Catch the ball with the fingertips. Balls below the waist can be caught with the hands and forearms.
5. Catch the ball as high off the ground as possible.
6. After catching the ball, bring it close to the body and cradle it in both arms for protection.

Distribution

When the goalkeeper obtains possession of the ball with her hands, it is her duty to initiate her team's attack. Too many goalkeepers give the ball away after

FIGURE 7.30
Catching a ball in the air

Table 7.18 Correcting Problems with Catching	
Problem	**Possible Causes and Solutions**
The player drops the ball after catching it.	The ball was not brought into the body and cradled with both arms. Bring the ball closer to the body for greater control.
The ball goes through the player's legs.	The legs were left open when catching and the ball was missed. When dropping to one knee, do not leave a space between the legs large enough for the ball to roll through. If catching a low ball in the air, keep the legs close together.
The ball bounced off of the goalkeeper's hands.	Use the fingertips to make the initial contact with the ball. Balls that hit the palms first may rebound away.

they receive it, and their team has to continue to defend. Explain to your goalkeeper how important it is that she gets the ball to one of her teammates. Goalkeepers *punt* the ball to get the ball far down the field to a waiting teammate. They *throw* the ball when they want to distribute to a nearby teammate. Throwing is usually more accurate than punting.

Players might punt the ball to start a breakaway or to relieve pressure if the opposition has mounted repeated attacks on the goal. Players should punt the ball with a target in mind. It is usually safer to punt the ball to the sides of the field rather than up the middle.

STEPS TO SUCCESS: PUNTING

1. Hold the ball in both hands in front of the body.
2. Take a two- or three-step run-up to gain speed and momentum and transfer the ball to the hand opposite of the foot being used for the kick (ball in the left hand for a right-footed punt).
3. Hold the ball in front of the body about waist high, with the arm outstretched.
4. Kick the ball with the instep of the foot. The ankle should be locked and the toe pointed.
5. Follow through above the waist and across the body. Try to generate enough power to lift the body onto the toes of the standing foot.

FIGURE 7.31
Punting

Table 7.19 Correcting Problems with Punting	
Problem	**Possible Causes and Solutions**
The player misses the ball.	The eyes were not on the ball, or the ball was tossed in the air prior to punting. Keep the eyes on the ball, and punt the ball out of the hand.
The ball goes high, but not very far.	The ball was held too high at contact. Adjust the position of the arms to hold the ball just below waist level when the ball is punted. The kicking foot should be traveling upward and outward when contact is made.
The player shanks the ball.	The side of the ball was hit instead of the center. Aim for the centerline of the ball.

Goalkeepers throw the ball when distributing to a nearby teammate. Unlike a throw-in when the ball is being restarted from the sideline, there are no rules governing the technique that the goalkeeper must use. While there may be many ways to throw the ball, the method used to obtain maximum speed is the sling throw.

STEPS TO SUCCESS: THROWING THE BALL

1. Hold the ball in the throwing arm by cupping the ball with the fingertips and hand against the forearm.

2. Take a two- or three-step run-up to generate momentum prior to releasing the ball.

3. Point the shoulder of the nonthrowing arm toward the target. Aim the ball so it bounces before it gets to the receiver. A bouncing ball is easier to control and will have slowed down.

4. "Sling" the ball at the target with a catapult-like motion by keeping the throwing arm straight (keeping the arm straight provides greater power) and by bringing the ball from the waist to over and past the head.

5. Release the ball as the arm passes the ear. Follow through down and across the body. The ball should travel on a straight

FIGURE 7.32
Throwing the ball

Table 7.20 Correcting Problems with Throwing	
Problem	**Possible Causes and Solutions**
The throw is arced instead of being a line drive.	The ball was released too early. Release the ball just after the hand reaches its highest point and is moving downward.
The throw is inaccurate.	The follow-through or body alignment was incorrect. Begin the run-up directly toward the target, have the nonthrowing shoulder pointed at the target, and follow-through directly at the target.
The ball has sidespin instead of backspin.	The ball was thrown from the side of the body rather than from over the top. Use a windmill-like motion with a straight arm for maximum power. Sling the ball from over the head with the hand as high as possible.

GOALKEEPING GAMES AND EXERCISES

Keeper Wars (U8 and older appropriate)

Goalkeepers play against each other in a 15-yard wide by 20-yard long field (adjust the length based on the size and strength of your players), with regulation goals on each end. Goalkeepers try to score on each other by finishing, punting, and throwing. If a save is made, the player may immediately attack the opponent's goal, but she may not take more than three steps prior to playing the ball. You can also restrict her to two touches. Who can score the most goals?

Toss & Save (U10 and older appropriate)

Play one keeper with a coach or partner. The partner is the server who tosses the ball to the keeper, whose job is to make a save. Tosses should include ground balls, balls directly at the keeper, balls in the air, and balls that require the goalkeeper to move. The ball may also be kicked at the goalkeeper. Use this exercise as a warm-up and to help improve the goalkeeper's catching technique. How many clean catches can the goalkeeper make in a row?

Finishing Games (U8 and older appropriate)

Any game that involves shooting on goal may also be used to coach the goalkeeper. Create activities that result in a shot on goal, and you also have an exercise that helps your goalkeepers.

line with very little arc and with backspin, which allows the ball to travel straight. Sidespin results in a curved ball.

SUMMARY

Although there are eight areas of technique in soccer, the many variations within each area result in an infinite number of ways that soccer players can work with the ball. A player can never become proficient at every possible technique, but should strive for improvement. Your role is to create opportunities for your players to practice technique while playing in an atmosphere that reflects the game. When teaching technique, use a progression. Employ exercises that allow frequent repetition of the required technique but that also pose a challenge. Approaching the game from its technical side will allow you to practice your player-development philosophy.

8

SCORE GOALS!

HOW TO TEACH SUCCESSFUL ATTACKING SOCCER

TACTICS INVOLVE THE DECISIONS that soccer players make during play with and without the ball and the actions they take based on those decisions. *Attacking tactics* are the decisions players make about which techniques to use and how to use those techniques when their team has possession of the ball. Attacking players who don't have the ball need to determine their best course of action to help their teammates who do have the ball. Two factors come into play when making attacking decisions: (1) the objective desired and (2) the ball's location on the field.

Tactical speed refers to the quickness with which players make correct decisions. Players improve their tactical ability when they increase the number of correct decisions they make and decrease the time needed to make those decisions. There are very few tactical differences between boys and girls. Soccer is soccer, regardless of who is playing.

The decisions that players make when choosing their actions are influenced by the number of players involved in the action. Tactics can be categorized as individual, small group, and large group. The player with the ball uses individual tactics. Those near the ball are involved in small group tactics. The entire team, including the players far from the ball, uses large group tactics. The attacking decisions that players make are also guided by a group of seven principles—

guidelines that help direct players toward the correct action. These guidelines are discussed later in this chapter.

When coaching players under the age of 13, a coach's priority is to train them to become tactically proficient individually and in small groups. The large group tactic that a coach should be most aware of when working with younger players is the arrangement of the team on the field, or the team's system of play.

TEACHING TACTICS

Tactics are taught similarly to technique. You should progress from a simple to a complex action. A player learns tactics through experience; the level of tactical understanding is related to the mental development of the players. Concentrate on improving your team's ability to maintain possession of the ball as individuals and in small groups. Any tactic involving three or more players is probably too complex for young players to understand, especially if they have not yet mastered working in pairs. Be patient when working with your team on tactics. Set up your technical exercises so that they require the players to make decisions, and you will improve your team's technical and tactical ability at the same time.

There are two approaches to teaching tactics: (1) The coach demonstrates and the players repeat, and (2) the players are placed in a situation and must decide what to do.

In the first approach, the coach sets up a situation and demonstrates the correct action for that situation. The players then perform

EVERYONE IS A TACTICIAN

Whenever people watch a sport, whether soccer or something else, they frequently assess a team's or an individual's decision-making skills. Sometimes a spectator might lament a technical error, or perhaps spectators will question a player's or coach's decision. Enthusiastic parents will encourage their daughters to shoot or dribble. They don't mean to interfere, but if you have been teaching your players to pass during a specific situation, and your players' parents are yelling at them to do something else, the players may become confused or frustrated. During your initial parents' meeting, explain to them that it is okay to encourage, but not to instruct. Let them know that in addition to teaching the players how to carry out the skills of soccer, you are also showing them what they should do in specific situations. It is in the players' best interest to let them play the game.

that action repeatedly. In this case, the players are not making decisions; instead they are working on performing the action. This approach is a good way to introduce a tactic and to reinforce its execution.

In the second approach, you place players in a situation and allow them to decide how to act. For instance, the players could practice 1 V 1 tactics by playing in a one against one game. The object is to beat the defender. The attacker decides how to achieve this goal on her own. When using this method, the coach establishes a goal and opposition and determines if the players are successful. Your decisions on when to provide feedback will become easy. If the players succeed, congratulate. If they do not succeed, correct. This approach is good to use when teaching about making the actual decision. However, players must have practiced the action before they can make the decision to use it.

Keep in mind that the object of the attack is to carry out some intent. It might be to score a goal, to get the ball into a certain area, or to complete a certain number of passes. If your players execute a tactic incorrectly, but the result of the movement is still successful, do not correct them. Tactics are about results. Correct your players if and when a decision proves unsuccessful.

GENERAL ATTACKING PRINCIPLES

Whenever a team has the ball, the objective is to maintain possession and to score a goal. As a coach, your job is to teach your players the principles they should use when attacking. During games and practices, analyze how well your team utilizes the following principles.

1. **Penetration.** Move the ball behind the defenders. An attacking team must get past defending players to score a goal. Individuals might penetrate with a dribble, or groups can penetrate by passing among each other to move the ball past the opponents.

2. **Depth.** Players should be available for support ahead of and behind the ball. Players without the ball need to provide passing options for their teammates. A team provides depth by getting the front players forward and keeping the back players behind the ball. A team's depth is defined as the distance between its frontmost and rearmost players (not including the goalkeeper). Depth should be maximized as much as possible. (See figure 8.1.)

Regardless of how far they are from the ball, players are described as being in front of, square with, or behind the ball. Imag-

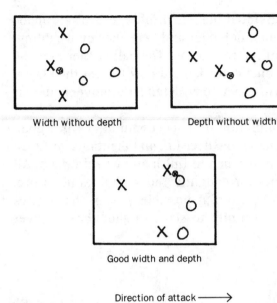

Width without depth   Depth without width

Good width and depth

Direction of attack ⟶

FIGURE 8.1
Combinations of width and depth

ine a line running from sideline to sideline that goes through the ball. Any players that are closer to the goal being attacked than to the line are in front of the ball. Players closer to the goal being defended are behind the ball. Players even with the ball are in a square position.

3. Width. Just as players should be ahead of and behind the ball to provide passing options, players should also be spread from side to side. When players spread out, teams can switch the point of attack (pass from side to side). Good attacking width also causes the defending team to spread out, creating openings that can be used for penetration. A team's width is defined as the distance between its two players who are furthest apart. (See figure 8.1.)

4. Mobility. If defenders could have their way, they would remain stationary. The principle of mobility is used to cause defenders to move. Attacking players who do not have the ball should run to make defenders move. Players running off the ball, both across the field and up the field, cause defenders to make decisions. If the defender runs with the attacker, a space is opened that the ball carrier or another attacker can use. If the defender does not choose to run with the attacker, the attacker may become open. Mobility can cause defenses to become unbalanced, which leaves some area of the field or attacker unguarded.

5. Combination play. Two or more attackers cooperate to move the ball by passing and dribbling. Combination play is the coordinated action of two or more players to penetrate the defense. Two-player combinations are very useful in beating a single defender. The players might pass between each other, or the ball carrier may use the teammate as a decoy and keep the ball. Regardless of the decision, the objective is to get the ball safely past a defender. Most combinations involve two players, but teams might try to combine with three players.

6. **Improvisation.** Individual players dribble to beat an opponent. When a player takes on a defender and beats her by dribbling, she has used the principle of improvisation. The ball carrier must be able to decide when to take on a defender and how to beat the player. Players use improvisation to react to a defender's movement that allows immediate penetration.

7. **Finishing.** The culmination of a successful attack is a goal. While finishing is also technique, the decision and mentality to finish is a tactic. Players need to know when to finish and when to pass. All the possession in a game goes for naught if the team does not score. Encourage players to finish as often as possible. A shot that misses the goal at least has an opportunity to score—a shot that is never taken does not.

The Thirds of the Field

The principles of attacking tactics are used no matter where the team has possession of the ball. However, their application depends on where in the field the ball is located. A field can be divided into

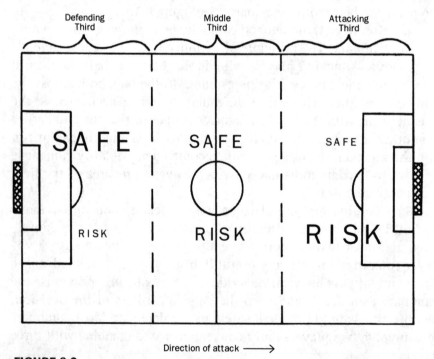

FIGURE 8.2
The thirds of a field

thirds: the defending third, the middle third, and the attacking third (see figure 8.2). Each third will affect the actions of the team and of individual players.

Decisions that players make involve some sort of risk. Low-risk decisions, in which success is probable, are highly safe. Passing the ball to a wide-open teammate or keeping the ball when under little or no pressure are highly safe. Decisions that could result in losing the ball, such as dribbling in a crowded area or passing to a marked teammate, are high in risk. Players need to be trained to make decisions with risk and safety levels that are associated their location on the field.

In the defending third, safety is the team's primary focus. Any ball lost in this area could result in an immediate scoring opportunity for the other team. All passes should be safe, and dribbling should be held to a minimum.

In the middle third, teams can become a bit more risky, but they still need to play safe. In the hopes of penetrating, players might choose to play passes that could be intercepted. Players shouldn't be too risky and should aim to keep possession, however, since the opponents could steal the ball and only have to beat a few players before attacking the goal. There should be a balance between dribbling and passing in the middle third.

In the attacking third, teams can become much more risky in their attempts to penetrate by dribbling and passing. A successful risk could result in high dividends (a goal). If the risk fails and the opposition obtains the ball, they are still very far away from their goal, and the attacking team will probably have most of its players between the ball and goal. In this space, players should look to dribble and shoot before looking to pass.

The actions in the different thirds of the field resemble actions in life itself. The key is to take risks where success will be worth it and the players can recover from failure. When the potential of failure outweighs the benefit, a safe approach is best.

INDIVIDUAL ATTACKING TACTICS

The decisions made by the ball carrier in a 1 V 1 matchup include when to finish, pass, and dribble. The player must be able to decide what kind of finish should be used and where to aim the ball. If passing is called for, the player must be able to determine who to pass to and what kind of pass is required. If dribbling is necessary, the ball carrier must be able to choose where to dribble, what kind of dribbling to use, or if the ball

TAKE THEM ON MENTALITY

The most exciting players are those who are willing to take the chance to beat defenders. This mentality might be natural, but it can also be trained. Encourage your players to take on opponents whenever appropriate. An ideal team consists of 10 players who possess the confidence and bravery to take the ball at defenders.

There may be times when a person who keeps the ball is called a "ball hog." There is a difference, however, between a ball hog and a "take-on artist." A ball hog is a player who gets the ball and has no intention of giving it up. She dribbles with their head down and usually keeps the ball until she loses it. A take-on artist, on the other hand, is a player who is willing to take the ball at defenders to create opportunities for herself and her teammates. The game of soccer needs more take-on artists. Protect and encourage your take-on artists, and try to develop this mentality in all of your players.

should be shielded. Players need to perform the required movement and choose quickly the correct course of action. Many times players make the correct decision for a situation, but because they took too long to make their choice, they were unsuccessful.

Individual tactics should be a major part of the training program for all ages. Penetration, improvisation, and finishing are heavily emphasized in individual tactics. Combination play may also be involved because the ball carrier must be able to choose a correct passing option when playing the ball to a teammate.

Defenders are beaten when an attacking player dribbles at them and changes speed, changes direction, or performs a combination of the two. Players should take on defenders any time the defender has space behind her. If there were another defender in the space behind the first defender, a better option would be to pass to a teammate, unless the second defender was so close that she would also be beaten with the fake. The amount of space necessary depends on the skill level of the players and on the method used to beat the defenders. Those who are proficient at keeping the ball near their bodies while faking opponents might not need as much space. Those who rely on speed to beat an opponent will need more area in which to dribble. As long as you set up situations that require players to use improvisation, they will learn through trial and error what works best for them.

Coaching Tip

1 V 1 games not only improve tactical and technical ability, but they also are a great source of fitness training. Replace sprinting activities with a 1 V 1 tournament involving everyone. Your team will benefit from the economical training.

STEPS TO SUCCESS: BEATING AN OPPONENT

1. Identify that open space exists behind the defender.
2. Dribble at the opponent's front foot.
3. When near enough for a fake to work but not so close that the ball can be stolen, perform a fake to cause the defender to lose balance.
4. Immediately after faking, accelerate past the defender.
5. Cut into the space behind the defender to shield her from the ball.

All of the games used to work on improving dribbling can also be used to work on individual attacking tactics. Use the games from chapter 7, or set up games involving 1 V 1 situations, to improve your team's attacking tactics.

SMALL GROUP ATTACKING TACTICS

Small group tactics involve the collective decision making of two or more players. While the ball carrier will always be able to utilize individual tactics, small group tactics usually depend on the actions of the players who don't have the ball. The concepts of depth, width, mobility, penetration, and combination play all are used in small group tactics.

FIGURE 8.3
Beating an opponent

At any time, a soccer game can be reduced by analyzing the field near the ball. The team with the ball is going to be in one of three situations: numbers-up (more attackers than defenders), even (equal attackers and defenders), or numbers-down (more defenders than attackers). When in a numbers-up or even situation, attempt to penetrate. When in a numbers-down situation, possess.

Teams that are able to develop numbers-up situations are usually very successful because they outnumber the defenders. Older teams are mentally capable of determining how to move the ball to find a numbers-up situation. Younger teams will have problems accomplishing this because of their limited ability to process information quickly. With players 13 and under, emphasis should be placed on how to recognize a numbers-up condition and what actions will work to penetrate past the defenders. Young players should also learn how to create a numbers-up situation when they have even numbers.

Coaching Tip

The easiest way to create a numbers-up situation is to dribble directly at a defender while a teammate moves near to help support.

2 V 1

In a numbers-up condition, any number of players might be involved. The simplest situation is two attackers against one defender (2 V 1). There are a variety of ways that teams may penetrate in a 2 V 1 situation. As with 1 V 1 attacking, there must be space available behind the defender to allow penetration. If there is no space, the players should not attempt to penetrate.

There are a variety of ways that two attackers can beat one defender, each involving the principles of penetration, mobility, and combination play. Each method forces the defender to make a decision. No matter what course of action the defender takes, the attackers are ready with an action that can be used to beat the defender. In every 2 V 1 tactic, the ball carrier always has the option to improvise and carry the ball past the defender. Each 2 V 1 movement causes the defender to choose either to (1) stay with the ball and block the dribble or (2) move between the ball carrier and the second attacker to block the pass. The attackers should move in a way that the defender cannot accomplish both. In all 2 V 1 situations, the attacker without the ball is referred to as the "supporting player."

The one-two, or wall pass, is best used when an attacker is carrying the ball up field and the supporting player is ahead of the ball. A midfielder might dribble the ball ahead, and a front player might come back toward the ball to support. The ball carrier passes to the supporting player, who returns the ball with one-touch to the passer. Between passes, the original ball carrier runs into the space behind the defender, who has chased the ball.

STEPS TO SUCCESS: ONE–TWO

1. Carry the ball directly at the defender.
2. The supporting player moves evenly with the defender off to an angle, far enough away that the defender cannot block both the pass and the dribble.
3. The ball carrier passes to the feet of the supporting player and runs past the defender on the other side.
4. The ball is returned to the original player in the space behind the defender.
5. If the defender blocks the pass, keep the ball.

An overlap occurs when the supporting player comes to help from behind the ball. A back player overlaps a teammate who has the ball. This means the back player runs around her back and past the teammate with the ball. Overlaps frequently occur on the outsides of the pitch and, because the supporting player is coming from behind, require communication. This move takes advantage of a defender's momentum. She might be coming toward the ball, while the overlapper is running past her. A pass into the space ahead of the overlapper will catch a defender moving in the wrong direction. There must be space behind and to the side of the defender for this move to work.

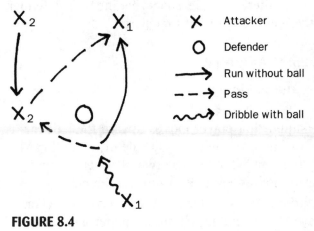

✕	Attacker
◯	Defender
→	Run without ball
--→	Pass
⌇→	Dribble with ball

FIGURE 8.4
One-two

STEPS TO SUCCESS: OVERLAP
1. Carry the ball directly at the defender.
2. The supporting player alerts the ball carrier that she is overlapping by yelling, "Hold." The ball carrier keeps the ball, but continues to move forward.

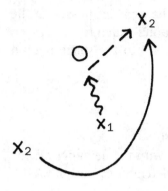

FIGURE 8.5
Overlap

3. The supporting player runs around and past the ball carrier, far enough that the defender cannot block both the pass and the dribble.

4. The ball carrier passes to the space ahead of the overlapping player.

5. If the defender blocks the pass, keep the ball.

Takeovers occur when two players crisscross in front of a defender. A takeover is much like a handoff. The player with the ball carries it at a supporting player, who runs past the ball carrier. The supporting player should run to the opposite side of the ball carrier of the defender. The ball carrier can let the supporting player take the ball, or she can keep it for herself. There must be communication between the two players to prevent the takeover from becoming a tackle. The move should occur with each player using the same foot (for example, right foot to right foot). Immediately after crisscrossing, both players should sprint away. Takeovers can put a defender off balance because she has to hesitate to see who ends up with the ball. This is a good move to use when moving across the field or when there is little space behind the defender because it can pull other defenders out of that space.

STEPS TO SUCCESS: TAKEOVER

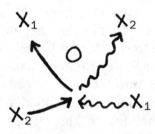

FIGURE 8.6
Takeover

1. Carry the ball into a space across the front of the defender, directly at a teammate.

2. The supporting player moves toward the ball carrier, running on the opposite side of the ball carrier than the defender. The two attackers should crisscross close enough to rub shoulders.

3. Just prior to crossing, the ball carrier says, "Take," or, "Leave." "Take" means that the supporter should take the ball. "Leave" means that the ball carrier will keep it.

4. Do not pass the ball. Let the supporting player take it off of the foot.

5. Both players should accelerate away just after crossing to take advantage of the off-balance defender.

A double pass might be thought of as two successive one-twos. The ball carrier plays the ball to a supporting player, who immediately returns it. The supporting player then runs past the defender

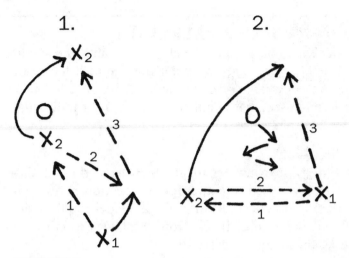

FIGURE 8.7

Two types of double passes: (1) Freeing a player and (2) Supporting a player even with the ball

and receives a pass from the ball carrier. This is an effective move when working to free a supporting player from a mark. It is also effective when the supporting player is even with the ball carrier.

STEPS TO SUCCESS: DOUBLE PASS (FREEING A PLAYER)

1. The defender is on the supporting player's back (between the player and goal).

2. The supporting player comes back toward the ball on an angle. Play the ball to the feet of the supporting player. Do not let the defender step around to intercept.

3. The supporting player passes back and immediately turns to run past the defender.

4. The ball carrier plays a one-touch pass into space for the supporting player.

STEPS TO SUCCESS: DOUBLE PASS
(SUPPORTING PLAYER EVEN WITH BALL)

1. Carry the ball toward the defender.

2. Play the ball to the feet of the supporting player.

3. Because the ball has not gotten past the defender, she will often move to the supporting player. Immediately pass back to the original ball carrier.

2 V 1 ATTACKING GAMES AND EXERCISES

When working on 2 V 1 attacking, players must be able to visualize the action to understand why it will be effective. Players under the age of 8 have not developed mentally enough to be capable of this process. Work on 2 V 1 tactics when the players are 10 and older. Let younger players master individual tactics and basic techniques.

2 V 1 grid work (U11 and older)

In a 15-yard-by-20-yard grid, allow players to practice the various 2 V 1 moves. Start the supporting player from the appropriate location relative to the ball for the movement being practiced. Restrict the defender to allow the action to occur. Then let the defender play freely. How do players react to the defender? Are they executing the action successfully?

Variation 1: Play to endlines. Attackers attempt to combine and then dribble the ball over the endline behind the defender.

Variation 2: Play to a goal. Place the grid 10–15 yards from a goal. Once the defender has been beaten, the attackers try to score a goal.

4. The supporting player should sprint into the space behind the defender to receive a pass. This move could be thought of as a one-two after a square pass.

2 V 2

Even number situations occur any time there are an equal number of attacking and defending players near the ball. The attackers should act quickly, using mobility and combinations play, to change the situation into a numbers-up situation. Penetration is always the ideal.

The ball carrier can eliminate a defender by dribbling directly at her and then passing to penetrate. A supporting player can eliminate a defender by running off of the ball. The defender might be enticed to follow the runner, thus providing space for the attackers. Although 1 V 1 is technically an even number situation, it could be addressed as a numbers-up situation because one attacker could easily join the ball carrier. Teams should look to create as many 1 V 1 duels around the field as possible.

STEPS TO SUCCESS: 2 V 2 ATTACKING

1. Carry the ball directly at a defender. The defender will do one of three things: (a) come toward the ball; (b) hold her position;

Variation 3: Counterattack. The defender plays 100 percent. If the defender can steal the ball and dribble over the endline from which the ball started, she scores a point. Rotate players so all get a chance being with the ball, supporting, and defending.

3 V 2 + 1 (U11 and older)

Play three against three in a 40-yard-by-30-yard grid. Place regulation-sized goals (made with cones if necessary) on each endline. The defending team drops one player into their goal to act as a goalkeeper, causing a 3 V 2 situation on the field. If the defending team steals the ball, they must pass back to their goalkeeper before they can attack. Play for 10 minutes. Many opportunities for combination play should occur. Do your players recognize a 2 V 1 situation?

3 V 3 + 2 neutral players

Play three against three in a 40-yard-by-30-yard grid with regulation goals. Add two players who will be "neutral"—they play with whichever team has the ball. Numbers-up situations will occur all over the field. Can your players recognize and act appropriately?

or (c) retreat. If the player retreats, continue to dribble and treat as a 1 V 1. If the defender comes toward the ball or holds her position, combine with a supporting player.

2. The supporting player runs to cause the second defender to move. Runs across the field (an unbalancing run) or up the field (a penetrating run) will result in the defender moving or the supporting player being open.

3. Play quickly to exploit slow decision making by the defenders.

SYSTEMS OF PLAY

The system the team decides to use is a series of numbers that describes the positioning of players on the pitch. Each number corresponds to a group of players playing similar positions. Positions in soccer are categorized as back players (fullbacks), middle players (midfielders), and front players (forwards). Teams may play with any number of players in each group, but usually distribute their players to ensure depth and width. (The numbers used never include the goalkeeper.) The numbers used in an 11-a-side system add up to 10.

When describing a system, a series of three numbers is used to state the number of backs, midfielders, and forwards, in that order.

For example, a 4-3-3 system has four backs, three midfielders, and three forwards. The numbers do not tell anything about how the players are aligned across the field, just from back to front.

2 V 2 ATTACKING GAMES AND EXERCISES

2 V 2 to Small Goals (U8 and older)

Two teams play on a 20-yard-by-30-yard field. Small (2-yard) goals are on each endline. Both teams line up behind their own goal. The coach has all of the balls and stands on one sideline. As the coach kicks the ball onto the field, two players from each team enter the field and play against each other. When the ball leaves the field, a new ball is played in and two new players from each team play. The former players move off the field quickly and rejoin their teams. Who can score three goals first? (See figure 8.8.)

3 V 3 tournament (U10 and older)

Play three against three to small goals on a small field (20 yards by 30 yards). Shots must be below the knees to count. Can the three with the ball work to establish quick attacks and unbalance the defense? Rotate teams so all play against each other. Who scores the most goals throughout the tournament?

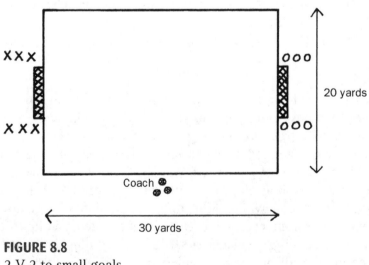

FIGURE 8.8
2 V 2 to small goals

11-a-Side

Many different systems are used by teams that play with 11 players. Each has its own set of strengths and weaknesses. Teams play in 4-3-3, 4-4-2, 3-4-3, and 3-5-2 systems. When selecting your team's system, choose a formation that best emphasizes your team's strengths and minimizes their weaknesses. Your system should have at least:

Coaching Tip

When a ball carrier dribbles directly at a teammate, the teammate should assume that a takeover could occur.

- 3 back players
- 3 midfield players
- 2 front players

Use the remaining two players in the positions that you feel will best help your team.

8-a-Side

When playing with eight players, the field is smaller, so depth becomes less important than width. As with the 11-a-side teams, use a system that best highlights your team's strengths. With seven field players, you might want to play with two lines instead of three. Typical systems include a 4-3, 3-4, and 3-2-2. Distribute your players so the team is always able to establish width and depth.

SUMMARY

During a game, players must make many decisions concerning the best course of action, both with and without the ball. The decisions that players make when their team is in possession are called attacking tactics, and these decisions are guided by a group of attacking principles. There are many ways to achieve the objectives stated by the principles—it is up to the players to determine the best way to solve the problem.

Regardless of how tactically sound a team may be, they will not be able to execute attacking tactics unless they are in possession of the ball. Technique always comes before tactics. Technique can be compared to having a car to drive, while tactics are the decisions made while driving. Without the car, there is no driving—without technique, tactics are useless.

9

STOP THE OTHER TEAM FROM SCORING

HOW TO TEACH SUCCESSFUL DEFENDING

A TEAM WILL ALWAYS be in one of two situations: Either it will or it will not have the ball. When in possession of the ball, the team is attacking, and their objectives are to keep the ball and score a goal. When defending, the team also has two objectives: to stop the opponents from scoring and to gain possession of the ball. The decisions that individuals and groups on a team make when the other team has the ball are known as *defending tactics*.

Defending is easier than attacking because it is easier to destroy than to create. When a team is defending, positioning and movements lead to success. With the exception of tackling, there is no reliance on technique. Many times, opponents can be forced to make mistakes or will make unforced errors that result in a turnover without the defending team making any attempted tackles. Your players should use correct tackling techniques, but they can still defend efficiently without tackling the ball.

As described in chapter 8, the attacking team moves the ball from its present location into the goal by passing, dribbling, and shooting. The number of people involved and the techniques used depend on a variety of factors, including the position of the ball and the nature of the opposition. All the actions in the sequence need to be completed successfully for the movement to end with a goal. The defending team, on the other hand, simply has to stop one of the attacking actions to be successful. When one part of the attacking sequence is destroyed, the entire action breaks down.

Another way to look at defending is: The attacking team has to get the ball through an area 8 feet tall and 24 feet wide (assuming the goal is regulation size); the defending team, on the other hand, is successful by getting the ball anywhere else in the universe! If the defending team can keep the ball from getting into a very small space, it is successful. In addition, defending to break up an attack does not even require that a technique be performed correctly.

As with attacking tactics, there is very little difference between the defending tactics used by boys and those used by girls. The only difference between males and females is in the positioning of players away from the ball. Because of size and strength differences, females are less likely to play a long ball from one side of the field to the other. When a girls' team moves the ball from one side to the other, it usually uses a series of passes rather than one long pass. For this reason, players near the ball can anticipate a pass to the player they are defending, and players away from the ball can drop in toward the middle. This difference, however, is very minor and is not a factor at all with younger players, who do not, whether boys or girls, possess the strength to play the long switching ball.

TEACHING DEFENSIVE TACTICS

Because attacking requires that players are proficient at keeping and controlling the ball, and defending is geared toward positioning, spend much more time working on attacking techniques and tactics. One defending session in every four or five practices should cover the subject enough to create a solid foundation for your players. Besides, any exercise that involves attacking will also involve defending.

As with attacking tactics, defensive tactics should be coached in a simple-to-complex order. Make things as simple as possible by using activities that involve 1 V 1, 2 V 2, or 3 V 3 match-ups. Even-numbered exercises

Coaching Tip
A small grid size will help defenders experience success, while a larger area will force them to make quicker decisions and will expose mistakes earlier.

are good when teaching defending, because the defenders match up equally with attackers.

Defensive coaching should focus on player positioning. The defenders' locations near and away from the ball will dictate the success of the team. The activities used to teach defending can be the same ones used to teach attacking. Rather than focusing on ball movement, however, focus on the defending team's positions and how they relate to the concepts of defending.

Whenever you teach defensive tactics to individuals or groups, adhere to the following guideline: *Do not confuse bad attacking with good defending!* The defender's primary job is to prevent her opponents from scoring a goal. Her secondary job is to gain possession of the ball. It is possible, and quite probable, that the attacking team will make technical or tactical errors that will result in them losing possession of the ball. The defending team then experiences success, but not because of anything they did. Be sure your players can differentiate between a great defensive play and a bad attacking play. It is not wrong to take advantage of a mistake made by the opposition. In fact, good defenders are patient defenders who wait for an opponent's miscue. But do not let your players believe that their actions forced the mistake.

When making a correction, use the freeze method to allow players to visualize where they need to be at a given time. When you call "Freeze" or "Stop," all players, attacking or defending, must stop in the exact location when the action was halted. Adjust any players who continued so they are back to where they were when the action was stopped. Then point out the incorrect positioning (or the correct positioning if making a point to reinforce) and explain why the player is in a bad (or good) location. If pointing out the incorrect positioning, move the players to the correct location and explain why that place is better. Allow play to continue from the ball's location when play was stopped.

It is also possible to use the freeze method to recreate a situation. The idea is to create a picture for your players so they can actually see where they need to be. In this case, freezing play would allow you to move players into locations where they were (or should have been) during a situation that occurred earlier. This approach is useful when

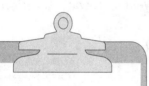

Coaching Tip

As players become more able to understand tactics, they will ask tactical questions about a specific situation. But these questions may be so specific that they apply to situations that might not occur again. Explain that actions should be guided by general defending concepts.

answering "what if" questions by the players or when reviewing possible situations that may not necessarily have happened.

DEFENDING RULES AND PRINCIPLES

Defending is more concerned with decision and movement than with technique. Before we discuss the various types of defenders, we'll first address rules and principles that make correct defending very easy.

The Golden Rules of Defending

When a team defends, there are two "golden rules" that should always be followed:

1. Always be goalside of the ball.
2. Be patient.

Goalside of the ball means that players should position themselves between the ball and the goal, so that they are available to defend. Any time a team loses possession, players need to move so they are nearer to the goal that they are defending than the ball.

The second rule of defending is to be patient. When a player defends against an opponent who has the ball, the biggest mistake she usually makes is to lose her patience. Overeager defenders attempt to win the ball by tackling at inappropriate times. When a defender tries to tackle and misses (also known as diving in), attackers are able to dribble past the off-balance defender. When patient, defenders slow down the opposition, which allows teammates to recover and help. It is better to stay between the ball and goal than it is to tackle and miss.

Although it is easy to write about having patience, teaching players this practice is difficult. Teach your players to tackle the ball only when the chances of winning it are very high, or when they know that they have a covering player ready to help in the case of a missed tackle.

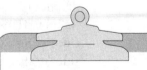

Coaching Tip

The concept of defending with patience is applicable no matter what age you are coaching. Players want the ball, and the idea of having patience must be reinforced constantly.

The Principles of Defending

As with attacking tactics, there are a group of guiding principles to use when defending. Defending principles and attacking principles are opposites. Everything that the attack is trying to accomplish, the defense is trying to prevent.

1. **Immediate chase.** When a player loses the ball, she should immediately pursue it and try to regain possession. It is common for players who lose the ball, whether through a bad dribble or mistaken pass, to put their heads down or be disappointed. But immediately after losing the ball is the time that the opposition is most vulnerable to losing the ball back, because they have to transition themselves from defending to attacking. Players who lose the ball should immediately try to win the ball back to take advantage of the opposition's reorganization.

2. **Control and restraint.** Defenders should be patient and tackle only when winning the ball is highly probable. The most common mistake made by defenders is the loss of control and restraint. An unsuccessful tackle often results in the attacker being able to penetrate with a dribble. Defenders who lose 1 V 1 confrontations often place their team at a great disadvantage because other players have to shift and leave their marks to defend against the attacker.

3. **Delay.** Defenders should establish a position goalside of the ball to slow down the opposition. Attackers try to penetrate the defense as quickly as possible. The faster they can get the ball past a defender, the less opposition they will encounter when going to goal. Because teams have players spread across the field, often when one defender is beaten, a group of defenders have been eliminated from the play. Therefore defenders should attempt to delay the attacker from penetrating, thus allowing teammates to fall back and get goalside. It also allows teammates to help defend the ball, or double-team the attacker.

4. **Cover.** The player who is pressuring the ball needs protection and help. Cover players position themselves behind the first defender (see figure 9.1). They aid in pressuring an attacker who dribbles past the first defender, and they also mark nearby attackers. This helps prevent defensive breakdowns caused by a dribbling attacker.

5. **Balance.** Players near the ball should step close to the players they are marking to delay and apply immediate pressure once the ball is passed, and possibly to intercept the pass. Players who are

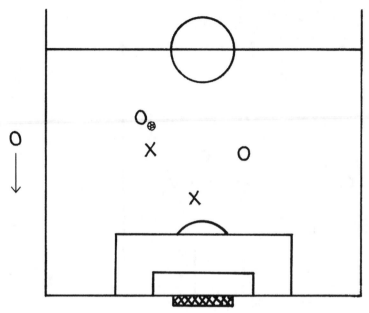

FIGURE 9.1
Example of a good cover position

marking attackers away from the ball should not be tight, but rather should drop in toward the space closer to the goal (see figure 9.2). This is the space where the attackers might run for a penetrating pass. The balance players should adopt a position that allows them to see the ball and the player they are taking care of at any given time. A good balance position gives defenders who are away from the ball the opportunity to guard against players who might be on the other side of the field. At the same time, the position allows defenders to help protect the middle of the field in case the defenders near the ball get beaten.

   6.   Concentration. Defenders should mass in the vital areas in front of the goal to limit the space available for the attackers, as shown in figure 9.3. Attacking teams try to spread the field using depth and width. Part of the reason for spreading out involves giving attackers more space to work with, but another part involves drawing defenders away from the spaces that attackers wish to use. Most goals are scored from central locations in front of the goal. When defensive teams concentrate, they fall back to defend the central areas of the field by reducing the amount of space the attackers can use.

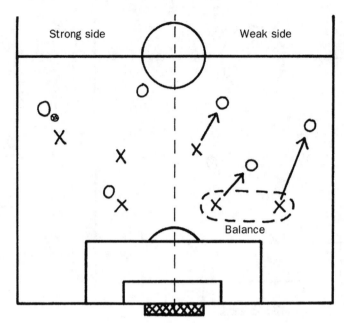

FIGURE 9.2
Example of good team balance

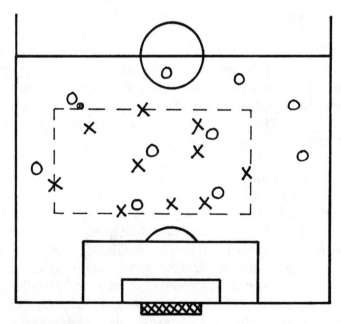

FIGURE 9.3
Concentration

FUNNELING BACK

When defenders retreat toward their own goal, they should funnel back. Players funnel back when they run toward their goal as opposed to toward the endline. Players on the wings should retreat back and to the middle of the field. They should take a path that is directly toward the near post (the goal post that is nearest to them). Central players can move straight backward. They will automatically concentrate in front of the goal.

7. **Communication.** The defending team needs to communicate so that their actions are coordinated and collective. While communication is important in all aspects of soccer, it is especially important when defending. Teams need to communicate to establish who will pressure the ball, who will mark the attackers, and where the player pressuring the ball should force the attack. A breakdown in defense can often be traced to a breakdown in communication.

DEFENDING ROLES

Just as the tactics used by attackers differ according to their positioning, so do the decisions of defenders. Players on the defending team are defined as the first, second, or third defender, based on their location relative to the ball (see figure 9.4). The *first defender* is the person who is nearest to and is directly responsible for defending the ball. The *second defenders* are those players who are close to the ball and are responsible for helping the first defender. There may be several second defenders. The *third defenders* are those players who are further away from the ball. Their job is to balance the defense and to track, or *mark,* attackers who are trying to get open. All of the defenders who are away from the ball are considered to be third defenders. Categorizing players as first, second, and third defenders helps to simplify the responsibilities of all players on the field at any given time.

First Defender

The first defender is the player who is directly defending the ball carrier. The principles of immediate chase, control and restraint, and delay are used by the defender nearest the ball. At any given time, the first defender is the most important player on the defending team

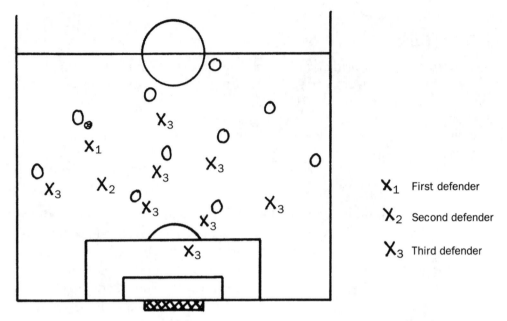

FIGURE 9.4
First, second, and third defenders

because she is directly responsible for stopping the advancement of the ball. Effective play of the first defender involves the proper use of the four P's:

- Pressure
- Predictability
- Positioning
- Patience

When a player pressures the ball, she positions herself goalside of the ball carrier and works to delay and deny penetration. The pressuring player might tackle the ball, but her most important duty is to prevent the ball carrier from moving forward. She needs to be near enough to cause the ball carrier concern about maintaining possession, but not so close that she can easily be faked. A good distance is about 1–2 yards, but will vary depending upon how far the ball is from the goal. The closer the ball is to either goal, the tighter the pressuring player.

Successful pressuring should be measured by denying penetration, not by winning the ball. Many times, defenders attempt to steal the ball at inopportune times, resulting in a missed tackle. Any time the first defender is beaten is a vulnerable time for the defensive team, because other defenders then have to move to the ball. This can result in attacking players being open and allows further penetration by the attacking team. Problems are compounded by spectators who encourage the defenders to win the ball rather than be patient.

Making the attackers choose an action that can be anticipated helps increase the chances of stopping the attacking movement. The pressuring player can make play predictable in two ways:

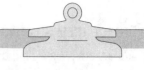

Coaching Tip

Informal conversations with parents about the importance of patience can help them to understand their daughter's intent when defending and can help reduce their "encouragement" to get the ball.

1. Approach (close down) the ball carrier with a curved run.
2. Stand goalside, but off to one side, to encourage the attacker to dribble to the other side.

When a defender moves to the ball, she is closing down the ball. Defenders usually have to get from their present positions to the ball carrier before they can pressure the ball, so speed is important. The faster the defender can begin pressuring the ball, the less time the attacker has to make a decision for action. Players should cover as much distance as possible with a sprint, but should slow down to regain control when nearing the ball carrier to guard against being beaten with a quick burst of speed.

Predictability can be established for other defending teammates by approaching the attacker on a curved run. If the defender can make a slight curve when approaching the ball, as shown in figure 9.5, the other defenders anticipate the direction in which the defender is going to try to force the attacker. The pressuring player can choose the direction of the curve, but it is more preferable for a fellow defender to direct the pressuring player because the pressuring player might not be able to see which direction is the best choice. The curved approach should be big enough to make it obvious which side the attacker is going to be forced to, but not so big that it gives the attacker more time to make a decision.

Forcing in this direction

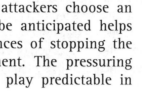

FIGURE 9.5
Closing down with a curved approach

FORCE THEM SOMEWHERE

Attackers possess the ball and are free to choose their actions. Defenders usually wait to see what the attackers attempt before they respond. Attacking is mainly proactive, while defending is mostly reactive. Anything that defenders can do to anticipate the attacker's actions will increase their chances to win the ball. Attackers usually try to get the ball to the middle of the field to increase scoring chances. If defenders force attackers to dribble and pass outside, not only can the defending team anticipate and act, but the attackers are also taken into a space that is less useful. Defenders should use the sidelines as extra defenders because they are another source of pressure. If not forced in one direction or the other, the attacker is likely to surprise the defenders because the defenders are unable to prepare for the attacker's actions.

Once she gets near the ball, the pressuring player should be positioned to make it readily apparent to teammates the direction in which the attacker will most probably dribble or pass the ball. If the pressuring player stands directly in front of the attacker, the attacker may choose to dribble to either side of the defender. If the defender, however, positions herself slightly to one side, the attacker is likely to try to dribble past the defender on the open side. The first defender is making play predictable and is allowing her teammates to anticipate the attackers' actions.

When pressuring the ball, assume a side-on position in which the front foot is nearer the ball and the back foot is further away (see figure 9.6). A side-on stance allows the defender to see both the ball and the space where she is forcing the attacker. If the attacker beats the defender with a burst of speed, the defender is already turned halfway and will be able to pursue more quickly. The defender should have her weight on the balls of her feet, with her knees bent, and should try to keep her center of gravity

FIGURE 9.6
Side-on stance

low. At no time should the defender come to a complete stop; rather she should keep her feet active to help when reacting to the attacker's changes of direction.

A defender jockeys by staying between the attacker and the goal as the ball carrier dribbles forward. The defender should remain in a side-on position and should shuffle backward instead of backpedaling. The defender should stay low and should never cross her feet. Jockeying keeps the attacker under pressure and slows down the attack. The defender should focus on the midsection of the ball carrier to help reduce the chances of falling for a fake, and she should be alert to any instruction from fellow defenders.

Players pressuring the ball naturally want to win the ball, but they need to be patient—a concept addressed throughout this book. The first defender is the player who must exhibit this characteristic most. Because players want to touch the ball, teaching defenders patience is a very difficult and time-consuming process. A good guideline to enforce is to not allow a pressuring player to tackle until a covering player tells her to.

STEPS TO SUCCESS: THE FIRST DEFENDER

1. Get to the ball carrier as quickly as possible while maintaining control. An approach that is too fast may allow the attacker to use the defender's momentum against her.

2. Approach the ball carrier with a curved run to make play predictable early.

3. Pressure to one direction by standing slightly to one side of the attacker.

4. Stay low to make changing direction easier. Keep the feet moving at all times.

5. Patience, patience, patience! Let the attacker make a mistake. Tackle only when the chances of winning the ball greatly outweigh the chances of missing the ball.

The Second Defender

The second defenders are the players who are in the immediate vicinity of but are not actually pressuring the ball. There are usually one or two players who assume this role. They should be positioned goalside of the ball, behind the first defender. The responsibilities of the second defenders are

- Covering
- Marking and tracking supporting attackers
- Communicating

If the first defender is beaten with a dribble, the second defender should be able to quickly take over as the first defender. Because the second defender's primary job is to provide cover, second defenders are sometimes referred to as covering players. The second defender's positioning should be close enough to the first defender to provide help, but not so close that the attacker's dribble can beat both defenders at the same time (see figure 9.7). A distance of 5–10 yards behind the pressuring player is usually sufficient, but will vary depending on the location of the nearby attackers. The distance from the first defender will also vary depending on the third of the field in which the ball is located. The cover player should move nearer to the first defender as the attackers penetrate into the attacking third. The second defender should not be flat or even with the first defender. Two or more defenders who are flat will be beaten with one dribble or one pass.

The attacking team usually has players who may be used for support near the ball. The cover player should be in a position that allows her to see both the ball and the supporting attacker, while also allowing her to protect the first defender. If the ball is played to the supporting attacker, the second defender should immediately step up to pressure the new ball carrier, becoming the first defender. If the supporting attacker makes a run forward to receive a pass, the second defender is responsible for tracking the run. Tracking the run means

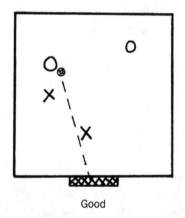

Good

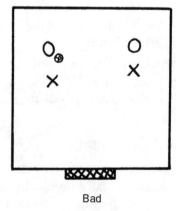

Bad

FIGURE 9.7
Correct positioning of cover player

the second defender runs with the attacker to prevent a successful pass or to apply immediate pressure on the receiving player.

Because the second defender can see both the attacker and defender, she should constantly be communicating with the first defender. The second defender can tell the first defender where to force the attacker. The second defender also needs to let the first defender know that she is there to provide cover. Without communication, the pressuring player must assume that she has no protection and has to defend safely.

STEPS TO SUCCESS: THE SECOND DEFENDER

1. Get in a position behind the first defender that allows immediate pressure on a penetrating attacker.
2. Keep track of players who are near the ball. See both the ball and the person at the same time.
3. If the ball is played to the supporting attacker, step up and immediately pressure.
4. Communicate with the first defender to inform her that she has cover.

The Third Defender

Third defenders are the remaining players who are not near the ball. Because there is usually one first defender and one or two second defenders, the remaining seven or eight field players (not including the goalkeeper) are third defenders. There are two categories of third

MAN-TO-MAN VERSUS ZONAL MARKING

Teams may use a man-to-man marking or a zonal marking system. When marking man to man, each defender is assigned a specific attacker to defend against. When using a zonal marking system, defenders are responsible for an area on the field, and their job is to mark any attacker who comes into that area. Each system has its pros and cons. Man-to-man marking is easier to understand, but can lead to problems if a defender loses her mark. Zonal marking helps clog up vital areas, but is more difficult to implement because the defender's mark will change as attackers enter and leave their zones of responsibility. Regardless of the system, the principles of pressure, cover, and balance still apply. A team must have a solid understanding of the concepts of cover and balance to use a zonal marking system successfully.

defenders: those who are on the strong side of the field, and those who are on the weak side of the field. If the soccer field were divided in half lengthwise, the side of the field where the ball is located is the strong side, and the opposite side is the weak side. The third defenders' responsibilities are

- Marking and tracking runners
- Providing balance
- Providing concentration

Third defenders on the strong side of the field should mark their opponents tightly because attackers on the strong side are more likely to receive a pass. Third defenders on the weak side of the field can drop toward the middle of the field and take care of opposing players more loosely than those on the strong side. Although the terms "marking" and "taking care of" are sometimes used interchangeably, it might help your players better understand their positioning if you use the terms to describe different actions. *Marking* implies staying very close to the opponent. A player might mark another player by being within a few yards of her. A player *takes care of* another player, however, by keeping track of that person, not necessarily by being close to that player. The distance that the defender can be from the attackers is relative to her distance away from the ball. The closer the ball, the closer the defender needs to be to the attacker. No matter what, however, the defender should adopt a goalside and ballside position (a ball side defender is nearer to the ball than to the opponent). She should also be near enough to be able to apply immediate pressure to the attacker receiving a pass.

The biggest mistake that third defenders make is letting attackers get open in spaces behind the defense. The defenders become guilty of "ball watching" and lose track of the running attackers. Just as the second defenders must stay with supporting players who run forward, third defenders need to track runners who make runs away from the ball, while at the same time keeping an eye on the ball. Penetrating runs and runs across the field are dangerous. By adopting a goalside position prior to a run, the third defender is already in the space that the attacker may attempt to use. If an attacker runs into an offside position, keep track of her but do not drop back to keep her on side. Use the offside rule as an extra defender.

Third defenders take care of players, but their main concern is to mark a space on the field that the attackers might try to use. They work to prevent long passes across the field that may end up behind

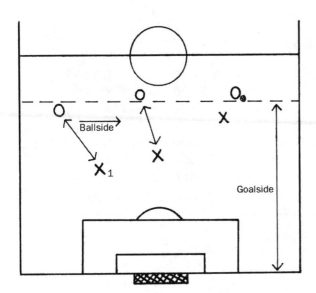

FIGURE 9.8

Proper balance and ballside marking (X_1 and X_2 are ballside and goalside of the attackers.)

the defenders. By doing so they provide balance on the weak side of the field while keeping track of players who do not have the ball (see figure 9.8). Balancing players might be better described as "loose" markers because they do not need to tightly mark the opponents away from the ball. When defenders balance, they fall in toward the middle of the field, while remaining goalside of their opponents. Balancing defenders should also be ball side of the player they are taking care of. By positioning themselves goalside and ball side, defenders are able to pick up attackers as they run toward the goal and be in a position that allows a possible interception of a pass. A balanced defense has players positioned to quickly pressure any passes to the weak side, but also to deny through passes that the attackers may attempt to penetrate the defense. The defense needs to be compact, but also ready to guard against the attacking team switching the ball to the other side of the field.

As the opponents move nearer to their goal, defenders away from the ball should tuck in and mass centrally. Allow the opponents to go outside, but try to keep them from bringing the ball inside. When players funnel back and balance, they automatically concentrate and clog vital goal scoring areas.

STEPS TO SUCCESS: THE THIRD DEFENDER

1. Always be able to see the ball and the opposing attacker.
2. Mark strong side players tight. Drop off and take care of weak side players.
3. Do not let attackers run into spaces behind defenders. Use the offside rule as an extra defender.
4. When in the defensive third, tuck in and concentrate near the middle of the field. Encourage attackers to move outside and away from the goal.

DON'T LET ATTACKERS GET AWAY WITH IT

When teams have the ball, they use attacking tactics to create goal-scoring opportunities. Many times the team that is better at disrupting the opponent's attack and defense is the winning team. One attacking principle is mobility. Attackers make runs off of the ball to get open and to unbalance the defense. The defending team wants to maintain balance. When teaching attacking, have your team make movements that pull balancing players out of position to expose space for other attackers. When teaching defending, explain to your team the need to maintain balance. Explain that the opposition is making runs to destroy the team's balance. This "reverse psychology" approach can help your players better understand why they need to work together when defending.

DEFENDING SET PLAYS

Free kicks and corner kicks present specific defending situations that allow defenders to organize. Before a free kick or corner kick, play stops. This stoppage of play gives the defensive team time to set up, thus reducing the chance of the opposition scoring. Teams use a wall to defend against free kicks that result in a shot on goal. During corner kicks, teams should organize themselves to reduce the amount of space that attackers have to create a goal-scoring chance.

Coaching Tip

Although rules state that no defensive player can be within 10 yards of the ball during a free kick, the attacking team does not have to wait until all defenders have moved away. They can restart the ball while the defenders are moving, and possibly surprise them.

Setting Up a Wall

A defensive wall is used to block a portion of the goal. Teams should set up a wall any time the opposition is near enough to the goal to attempt a shot. A wall consists of one or more players. The number of players in the wall depends on the location of the ball and the distance from the goal. Rules state that the wall can be no closer than 10 yards to the ball.

Five players should form a wall to obstruct a shot from the middle of the field (see figure 9.9). One player can drop off the wall as the ball's location moves nearer the sidelines. Two or three players should defend free kicks from the side of the penalty box. Players who are not in the wall are responsible for tightly marking the remaining opponents. When forming the wall, the players should stand shoulder to shoulder, facing the ball. The wall should be arranged so the player on one end is directly between the ball and the near post. The remaining players should be blocking the near side of the goal. The goalkeeper can then position herself to guard the far side of the goal and should move to see the ball before it is kicked.

Coaching Tip

Place your taller players on the side of the wall that is guarding the side of the goal that is furthest form the goalkeeper.

It takes courage to be in the wall, so make sure you select players who are willing to be hit with the ball and not move. You might want to select the wall players prior to the game. If a player moves or flinches when in the wall, a hole may result for the ball to go through. As soon as the ball is kicked, the players can move, but they should remain still until the shot reaches them.

There are two types of free kicks that are defended with a wall. During a *direct free kick,* the defenders should anticipate a shot on goal, but should mark nearby attackers tightly. The attackers might try a trick play to fool the defenders into moving, so it is important that the wall players are disciplined and stay put until the shot is taken. During an *indirect kick,* two players must touch the ball before a goal can be scored. The defenders should anticipate a pass prior to a shot on goal. It is wise to place one or two players near the wall who will rush the ball immediately after it is touched. These players should not be a part of the wall. Train the players to know the difference between the referee's signals for each type of kick (during an indirect kick, the referee holds one arm straight in the air until the ball has been

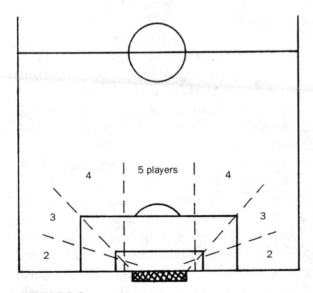

FIGURE 9.9

Amount of players to use in a wall based on the location of the free kick touched by a second player) to help them make correct decisions quickly.

Defending Corner Kicks

When defending a corner kick, use a mixture of zone marking and man-to-man marking (see figure 9.10). One player should stand 10 yards from the ball to serve as a wall. Her job is to cause the kicker to aim further away from the goal, which results in the defensive team having more time to act. Place a player on each goal post. Their jobs are to make the goal smaller for the goalkeeper by clearing any shots that might go into the corners. Most teams try to have their kicker aim for the top corner of the 6-yard box nearest the kicker, so place a player there whose job is to clear any ball in that area. The rest of the players should mark man to man against the attackers: They should stand so they can see the ball and the attacker and should be nearer the goal than the attacker. Markers need to move with the running attackers and attempt to anticipate the attackers' actions. Once the ball is kicked, the defenders should swarm to the ball.

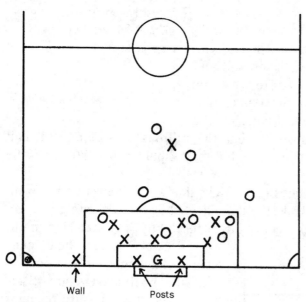

FIGURE 9.10
Defending a corner kick

The first duty of the team should be to clear the ball away from the goal. Try not to clear the ball over the endline, which results in another corner kick. However, do so if that is the only option available. The players on the posts should stay in place until the ball is cleared or until an attacker receives the ball but has to turn and shield. Train your goalkeeper to understand when the post players should move out and to issue the command for them to leave. Once the ball is cleared from the penalty box, all defenders should rush forward and out of the box. This will cause any lingering attackers to be offside if the ball is played back toward the goal.

PLACE TALL PLAYERS NEAR THE GOAL

Use the taller players on the team as the post players and as the player on the corner of the 6-yard box. Short players will not be effective on shots toward upper corners. Most corner kicks are played in the air, so a tall player on the corner of the 6-yard box will have a better chance of clearing the ball with her head. Players in these positions often have to defend by reaction, and many times do not have the chance to choose their action.

SUMMARY

In general, defending is easier than attacking because technique is not really an issue. Teach players to be goalside of the ball at all times. Work on pressuring, covering, and balancing to help your players defend as a team. Good defensive teams have and use appropriate plans during restarts. Many times, plans can be explained with a short talk during a training session prior to a game. Most important of all, train players to be patient when defending. More often than not, players win the ball because the opponents give it away.

Coaching Tip

Train your goalkeeper to call "Keeper" as she is moving to a ball that she can catch. Often the keeper call itself will cause the attackers to slow down because they are reluctant to collide with the goalkeeper.

10

TEAM MANAGEMENT

MOST COACHES WILL AGREE that the best part of their job is being on the field with the players. Planning and implementing training sessions and coaching during games are just a part of a coach's duties. The coach must also be able to manage a team on and off the field throughout the entire season.

Effective team management comes down to three things: preparation, organization, and communication. An effective coach prepares in advance for every training session, meeting, and game. All practices should have a theme, all meetings should have a purpose, and actions before and during games should follow a common plan. When preparing, be as organized as possible. Little things like planning the size of practice grids or the amount of time to spend on a specific exercise will help your practices flow. Have an agenda when meeting with your players' parents and stick to it. Decide during games where you will take the team for halftime and what you will tell them. Finally, always keep the avenues of communication open between yourself and your team. Let your team know in advance about games, practices, and schedule changes. Be open to comments and suggestions from others. If you communicate well, your team management will become much easier.

TRYOUTS

The first contact that many coaches have with their players is during tryouts. Teams are formed in a variety of ways. Some leagues have policies that do away with tryouts. Players simply sign up and are assigned a team and a coach. (Coaches often get "drafted" in these leagues.) Other organizations might have age-group tryouts. Every player of a given age participates and is then assigned to a team within the age group. Individual teams might also run tryouts. In this case, interested players attend one or more tryout sessions and attempt to make the team.

In a tryout, it is important that you be able to assess each candidate's ability to play the game of soccer. Plan the tryout so that it contains activities that will help you appraise the individuals' abilities in each of the four areas of technique, tactics, fitness, and psychology. If possible, have two or three tryout sessions. It is difficult, especially if there are many players at the tryout, to assess each player in one session. A multiple-session tryout will give you additional insight about the players and confirm your initial judgments. It is a good idea to enlist the aid of an assistant coach and perhaps one or two guest evaluators to help assess the players. Many times, one coach may see something that another coach misses. Extra opinions can help confirm selections or raise questions that help rate the players more accurately.

A tryout can be run very similar to an actual training session. The difference between the two, however, is that during a training session, coaching and teaching occur. During a tryout, coaching can take place, but the emphasis should be on letting the players perform. Get the players into situations that allow the evaluation of their soccer skills. If possible, have a guest coach run the tryout to give the head coach and assistant coach the opportunity to focus on evaluating the athletes.

A good tryout format includes:

- Individual ball control exercises
- Exercises that assess players during match conditions
- Small-sided games

The tryout session should be similar in length to an actual practice session. Provide plenty of soccer balls, or better yet, require each candidate to bring her own ball, shin guards, and water. Break the session into four parts of equal length. Use a quarter of the tryout for individual exercises, a quarter of the tryout for match condition exercises, and half the time for small-sided games. Small-sided games are better than a full-field scrimmage because each player gets more opportunities to touch the ball, which allows you a better chance to evaluate her. If any physical testing, such as running speed or jumping height, will be executed, schedule it during the middle of the session after the players are warmed up.

Make sure you assess players' overall ability. Prior to the initial tryout, a short explanation of the tryout session and the evaluation criterion will help answer players' questions. Expect players to be nervous, especially if there are many players trying out for a few positions. When evaluating, it is effective to answer the following questions about each player or to rate her in the following areas. (*Note:* Physical fitness should only be a major criterion when the players have completed puberty.)

TECHNICAL ABILITY

- Is the player comfortable with the ball?
- Does the player possess a mastery of basic techniques?
- Is there a specific technique (dribbling, passing, heading, shooting) in which the player excels?

TACTICAL ABILITY

- Does the player make good decisions when in possession of the ball?
- Does the player make good attacking decisions when moving off of the ball?
- Does the player understand the concepts of pressure, cover, and balance when defending?

PHYSICAL FITNESS

- How fast is the player?
- Does the player possess adequate endurance?
- Does the player possess a dominant physical attribute (exceptional speed, jumping ability)?

PSYCHOLOGICAL ASPECTS

- Is the player vocal?
- Does the player follow directions?
- Is the player a leader among the other players?
- How is the player's self-confidence?

SHOULD POSITIONS COME INTO PLAY DURING TRYOUTS?

A full team requires players for a variety of positions. On an ideal team, each player, whether back, middle, or forward, would be a good all-around soccer player. There are two approaches that coaches can take when selecting players. They can select players based on the positions, or they can select players whom they feel are the best soccer players. When selecting players based on position, the candidates can be divided and assessed against the others trying out for that position. When selecting players for their overall soccer abilities, the coach should have an idea of where that player will play if she makes the team. Either approach works well, but the evaluators should discuss the tryout philosophy with the candidates prior to the selection process.

Use these questions only as a guide. Add or eliminate evaluation areas as you see fit. Keep in mind that the purpose of the tryout is to determine the abilities of each player under equal circumstances. All players should be given the opportunity to offer her best effort for the evaluators.

PRESEASON

Once you have your team, you'll need to do some planning prior to the start of the season. Spend some time organizing for the upcoming season, and you'll avoid problems later.

Rosters and Phone Trees

After the members of the team have been established, prepare a player roster that includes each player's name, address, city (if necessary), parents' names, phone number, and e-mail address (if e-mail is going to be used as a method of communication). The player roster should be easy to read and should be provided to all players on the team. Your team can use the information to contact each other when necessary.

There are many times that you will need to get information to all of the team members, and there are many ways to distribute the information. One efficient method is to construct a phone tree in which each person is responsible for contacting another player or two. The last player or players on the list call the coach to help ensure that the phone tree was followed and the message was communicated accurately. This will reduce the number of phone calls that you will have to make and will help get the information out to team members more quickly.

An e-mail group can also be constructed. Because e-mails might not be checked on a regular basis, however, this method is better used for long-range announcements (such as a tournament or league schedule). Information about a change or addition that is occurring soon is better transmitted by telephone.

Practice Schedules

Establishing your team's practice schedule may be a simple task, but it's one that should not be overlooked. If your league or club has an arrangement with a local park or soccer complex, you may have a training location and time assigned to you. On the other hand, you might need to reserve a practice location for your team on your own.

Plan for at least two training sessions per week. You can have three or more practices each week, in addition to the regular game, but this is not necessary for players under the age of 12. The goal should be to have enough time to work on teaching and improving technique, but not so much time that practices could cause player (and coach) burnout.

Practice for about as long as an actual game lasts. U9s should train for about an hour at a time. U10s to U12s can work for about an hour and a half. Do not mistake quantity for quality. A well-planned 90-minute training session during which everyone is active is much more effective than a poorly planned 2-hour practice. Schedule training sessions at the same time on the same days each week to help establish a routine. Take into account your personal schedule and any transportation issues affecting your players.

Tournaments

There are many weekend tournaments for youth soccer teams. Prior to the season you should determine which tournaments, if any, you plan to enter. It is not a requirement to play in a tournament, but many players enjoy the opportunity to play in a weekend event against other teams from other leagues, with the chance of winning a championship.

Use caution when determining your team's tournament schedule. Much of what your team will be able to do depends upon their age, competitive level, and level of commitment. For younger players and beginning teams, a single tournament to end the season is probably

WHAT ABOUT TRAVEL?

Soccer tournaments are held across the country every weekend of the year. You might have access to a significant number of local tournaments, but most probably you will have to travel if you plan to play in many tournaments.

The purpose of tournaments is twofold. For the player, it provides an opportunity to play against other teams. For the sponsoring group, it is a chance to raise money. Many clubs sponsor tournaments to help finance their operations. This is great for the players in that club, because the funds generated often help defray the cost for each player. Traveling to an out-of-town tourney can help players deal with playing away from home, and often allows the team to compete against teams that it normally does not play. Travel, however, is probably not necessary until the age of 11 or older (unless your team is in an area that does not have local tournaments). One out-of-town tournament per year is probably enough. When choosing to play in an out-of-town tournament, however, have a reason for doing so. Explain to the parents why you feel it is important.

enough to satisfy the team. As the players become older and more experienced, you might want to enter two or three tournaments.

Tournaments cost money, so take into account the team's finances when selecting events. Tournaments that are held out of town require travel and lodging in addition to the entry fee. The decision to enter an out-of-town tournament should be based on the competitive level of the team and should be discussed with parents prior to making final decisions.

Preseason Parents' Meeting

A preseason meeting with your players' parents is important for establishing clear and open communications and for defining the expectations of the members of the team.

Your team's parents are your most important resource. They are responsible for getting their children to and from practices and games, and they can help perform the numerous tasks required during the season. Explain to parents at the meeting how important their role is to the success of the team.

Keep in mind that although you are concerned with the welfare of each player on your team, parents will be more occupied with the happiness of their own child. This is to be expected, and it needs to be dealt with by letting parents know that you will not play favorites.

During the parent meeting, outline your philosophies and goals for the season. Let parents know the team rules so they understand what is expected of their children and themselves. When you explain your views prior to the start of the season, you help parents understand your goals and prevent later problems.

Establish guidelines for players' parents. Explain to the parents your expectations about their actions during the season and during games. Some of your players' families might be participating in an organized sport for the first time. Some may have experience in athletics but might not have the same philosophies or expectations as you. Some of the issues that you need to address include:

- **Behavior during games.** All parents should be encouraging during games. There is no room for criticism of coaches, other players, the officials, and the other team. If you wish the parents to sit in a particular location, explain where and why. Many times it makes good sense to have the parents seated slightly away from the team. Overeager parents can crowd the bench, causing distractions to the players and difficulty for the players to hear the coach's comments.

- **Arrival on time for training.** It is most likely that parents provide your players' transportation and are probably at fault for a late arrival. Let parents know that timeliness is important. Don't blame the child for the parent's mistake.

- **Approximate costs.** Have a team budget ready so you can explain the costs of playing on the team. In addition to registration fees and the cost of uniforms, there may be other fees that the parents will be responsible for. Let parents know how much they should expect to pay for the season.

COACHING YOUR OWN CHILD

It is very possible that you may coach your own daughter. This can lead to some uncomfortable situations. It is easy to treat your child differently from the other players. Some coaches unknowingly favor their daughter by being less demanding or by allowing her to play certain positions ahead of other players. On the other hand, coaches might try to compensate by being overly hard on their child, holding her to a higher standard than they do the other players. When working with your own daughter, try to treat her as a player on the field, but as your daughter away from the game. Chances are that your daughter might also experience greater stress than the other players because she is trying to please you. It is important that you recognize her efforts after the games and practices.

GET THE PARENTS ON YOUR SIDE

Your players' families can be your greatest allies, or they can be your biggest source of complaints. Getting the parents to understand your approach, expectations, and philosophies will help to alleviate problems before they start. Keep the lines of communication open, and involve the parents in the administration of the team. Establish a line of authority, however, and let the parents know that they are expected to respect your decisions. If the parents are working with you instead of against you, you will find coaching to be a very pleasant and rewarding job.

- **Snacks and water.** It is common to have water and halftime or postgame snacks for the team. You might want to establish a "treat schedule" that assigns the duty to a different family each weekend.
- **Equipment needed.** Each player will be responsible for providing her own equipment (shoes, shin guards, correct sized ball) for personal use. New players may not be aware of the equipment that they need in order to play. Let the parents know what each player should have, including the correct sized ball.

It is also a good idea to use the parents' meeting to delegate tasks by forming committees. When you assign jobs to each parent, not only do you reduce the amount of work that you have to do, but you also actively involve them in the workings of the team. Such tasks as planning for tournaments and travel, fund-raising, planning team parties, and organizing halftime or postgame treats can easily be accomplished by others.

Equipment

One final task to complete before the season begins is to obtain practice equipment. Make sure you have a sufficient number of field markers and practice bibs for the number of players on your team. Also have a supply of balls of the correct size. Flags and soccer nets are good items to use during practices and games. If you have to purchase these things yourself, make sure you build the expense into the cost for each player. A few dollars from each player should easily be enough to cover the equipment costs for an entire team.

PREGAME

Before each game, there are a few tasks that should be completed upon arrival at the field.

If possible, you should be among the first to arrive to the site. By arriving a few minutes earlier than the rest of the team, you will be able to establish a meeting location and make an assessment of the facilities. Once you arrive at the park, especially if the team is playing there for the first time, find the location of the nearest bathrooms. If playing on a hot or rainy day, find the nearest shade or shelter that can be used during the halftime talk. Make sure you know where the nearest phone is located (if you do not have a cell phone). If an injury were to occur, you must have a way to alert the proper medical personnel.

Perform a quick survey of the field and surrounding areas for anything that might be dangerous to the players. Remove any litter, dangerous objects, or items that could cause injury. Take note of any holes and ruts. Locate any sprinkler heads that might be protruding from the ground. If you feel that anything on the field could cause an injury, alert the referee, the other coach, and any official who might be supervising the field.

When playing on a league field where multiple games take place each day, and if your game is the first of the day, make a thorough examination of the field. A quick evaluation will probably suffice if games have been held prior to yours. The chances are greater that a field may be in disrepair if the game is used for only a game or two as opposed to being used for a series of games, but nevertheless it is always better to use caution and check the area.

Your team should arrive to the field at least 30 minutes prior to game time. An early arrival will give sufficient time to warm up and provides a buffer in case some of the players are running late. If the field is being used, find an open space on the side where the group can warm up. Another approach could be to meet at a prearranged location and then walk as a group to the field.

Pregame Talk

If you have been involved with sports in the past, you undoubtedly have heard the "Win One for the Gipper" story, or perhaps you have played for a coach who spoke to your team prior to a game. Girls respond to motivational talks as much as boys do, but unless the game is a special match, like a championship game for a league or tournament, you probably do not need to have a special talk prior to the game. Younger players especially are usually intrinsically motivated and do not need any special pep talks.

If you choose to give a pregame talk, deliver it prior to the warm-up. Get the players concentrating on the game when they begin to prepare, not when they begin to play. Most females will not respond to a rah-rah speech that appeals to their intensity and effort. Use your comments to bring to the players' attention any special details about the game or team being played. Appeal to their sense of duty to the team and how their performance can help everyone be successful. Keep the talk positive, short, and to the point. Your players are better served to spend time physically preparing for the game—they probably already know how important it might be. Be careful not to put additional pressure on the players.

Warm-Up

Once the field survey has been completed and you are satisfied that everything is in order, you can turn your attention to preparing your team physically and mentally for the game. Your team's pregame warm-up should be a routine that gets them ready to play in a real match. By the end of the warm-up, the players should have broken a sweat, have an elevated heartbeat, and be psychologically ready for competition.

Many times, players do not become completely focused on playing until the game begins. This can result in problems, because a team that is ready can take early advantage of an unprepared team. Stress to your team the importance of the warm-up and that the game begins at the opening whistle—not 10 or 15 minutes later. If you have a good warm-up that motivates the players and gets everyone involved, your team will usually be ready to play when the game begins.

There are many types of pregame activities and routines that you can use with your team. There is no perfect or single way that is best. You might have a routine that works well, or you might have to determine through trial and error the best way to prepare the team. In general, it is probably better to have a specific pregame ritual that is used only before a game to help the players associate the activities with a real match. When selecting your warm-up activities, try to include exercises that

- Allow individuals to raise their heart rates while touching the ball
- Give the players a chance to stretch
- Progressively move from individual to small-group or team activities

- Allow players to use techniques that they will use during the game
- Are performed at game speed
- Include some sort of finishing

Because the team will only have 15–25 minutes to warm up, two or three activities will probably be the maximum you'll be able to complete. When selecting exercises, try to choose those that will involve everyone. Keep in mind that an individual player often has a preferred activity that gets her ready to play, so allow a short amount of time in which players choose their own actions. Most youth players, however, are not sufficiently able to prepare themselves to play without some leadership, so do not expect the players to come up with ideas on their own.

A good warm-up usually has three to four parts. The amount of time spent on each section should be relatively equal, probably lasting 5–7 minutes each. An ideal warm-up will end about 3–5 minutes prior to kick off, which allows individuals to take care of any last-minutes needs (bathroom, tying shoes and adjusting uniforms, a drink of water) and gives you a chance to address the team one last time prior to kick-off. The four parts of the warm-up include:

1. Group running or stretching activity
2. Possession game
3. Individual or positional activities
4. Finishing

The first section of the warm-up should be the only one that does not include a ball. A group run that is stopped a few times for team stretching will work well. Stress the importance of looking like a team. Have everyone perform the same type of activity at the same time. Some teams run in two lines around the field. Others choose to run as a single line shoulder to shoulder across the width of the field. If your players are young or beginners, you can lead the run. If the players are older, or if a few players have demonstrated leadership, have them lead the activity.

Use different types of movements (jogging, side shuffles, skipping, jumping to pretend to head the ball, backward running) to help the body warm up completely and to work on coordination and agility. Stretching can be completed between movements. Try to organize this phase so movement and stretching are alternated, as opposed to one long running session followed by stretching.

Once running and stretching are completed, have the team play some sort of possession game. The game could be a team game, or several possession games could occur at the same time. Playing 4 V 2 or 3 V 1 will help the players move and work together while keeping the ball. The idea during this phase should be to allow players to have touches on the ball and to work with teammates. If possible, group players according to their positions so they are working with players who will be near them on the field.

After players have moved around and have started to perspire, have them break up into groups to work on any special activities they wish to perform. Encourage players to do some of the things that they have to do during the game. Backs could head the ball and practice long passes. Midfield players could continue to work on short passing and possession. Wide players could cross the ball, and forwards could shoot on goal. Let the players choose their activities, but provide them with some guidance.

End the warm-up by giving all players the chance to shoot on goal. Players should be allowed to have at least 2–3 shots each. Wide players can continue to cross balls to be finished. Backs should take longer range shots. Set up something that is organized rather than just having the team take arbitrary shots. A simple shooting exercise will work well during this phase.

WARMING UP THE GOALKEEPER

The goalkeeper is a specialty position that requires a slightly different warm-up. An assistant coach should work with the goalkeeper or goalkeepers away from the team during the first part of the warm-up. During the running and stretching phase, have the goalkeeper carry a ball. Have her bounce the ball, toss the ball in the air and catch, and roll the ball and then move quickly to pick it up. As with the field players, allow stretching to occur between movements.

After running and stretching, have the keepers work on catching balls that are tossed by a coach (you could also have the keepers warm each other up, but make sure they are supervised). Start with balls tossed directly at the player. Progress to balls on the ground, balls to the side, and balls in the air. Strive for repetition and balls that help increase the goalkeeper's confidence. Move on to playing balls to the goalkeepers with the feet. Time the keepers' warm-up so they are ready to face some live shots by the time the team is ready to break into individual activities. The team should provide part of the goalkeepers' warm-up.

Use the last few minutes prior to game time to allow players to finish last-minute preparations and to give any last-minute instructions. The team has just completed a period of activity that has elevated their heart rates and has gotten them ready to play, so try not to have the players stop moving for a long period of time. With practice and through trial and error, you will be able to time the end of the field warm-up perfectly.

DURING THE GAME

Soccer does not have time outs or stop and starts like most other sports. Halftime is the only time that you have the opportunity to speak to your entire team. This is the only time that you have their entire attention and can make large-scale changes or coaching points. You probably only have 5–10 minutes, however, to get your points across, so it is important that you are efficient and organized when using this time.

Use the game time to evaluate and analyze the flow of play. Try to limit the number of instructions that you provide to the players during the game. Although it may be difficult, allow the players to choose their course of action. Incorrect choices reveal practice topics for the future. If you must call out advice, keep it positive and short. Communicate in terms that are easy to understand.

When analyzing, you could categorize your points into attacking or defending comments. You could also make points that pertain to different positional groups or team actions in the various thirds of the field. Be sure to list things that are going well!

Stay in Control

It is very important that you maintain your composure during the game. Try to stop yourself from frequent instructions to the players

PICK IT UP!

In a television program that shows videotapes of humorous experiences submitted by the viewers, one clip made a great point about keeping instruction simple and understandable. A group of seven- or eight-year-olds was playing in a game, and the coach wanted the players to work a little harder. He yelled out to the team, "Pick it up!" The player nearest the ball bent over, picked the ball up, and looked at the coach. It was what the coach said, wasn't it?

and from questioning the calls of the referee. Many players will tune out a coach who is chattering nonstop on the sideline. Although the referees may make mistakes, chances are that the referee of your game will be a parent or younger person who is doing his or her best. Your complaints will not change the call, nor will they help the situation. Many team's parents will take on the personality of the coach. If you present yourself as an emotional wreck who patrols the sidelines, expect the parents to do the same. If you stay calm, chances are that the parents will also.

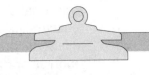

Coaching Tip

You might find it useful to have a notebook to jot down ideas and observations. Some of your comments will help you organize your halftime talk, and others will help you identify topics to practice later.

Make Purposeful Substitutions

Whenever you make a substitution, have a purpose in mind. Do not make a change just for the sake of making a change. You might choose to sub to rest some players. You might decide to make a change to alter a matchup on the field. Perhaps you have a policy that requires that each player be on the field for a certain amount of time. Regardless of the reason, have one in mind when changing players. Notify the substitute in advance that you will put her in the game so she can prepare. A few minutes of warming up will help the player be ready to play at full speed when she enters the game.

HALFTIME

Use the halftime interval to allow players to get a quick rest and some liquids. Water is best for halftime, although sport drinks are also good. Do not allow players to drink soda before the game or at halftime; the carbonation could upset their stomachs. A snack that is high in simple sugars, such as a piece a fruit, is good for replenishing energy. While the players are getting their water and snack, organize your thoughts with your assistant coach to plan the points you will make to the team during your halftime talk. Let players know as they come off of the field where they should go to sit for the talk.

For the halftime talk, you probably will be able to come up with a number of coaching points to share with the team. Psychologically, however, the players cannot handle more than two or three ideas at one time. If you're working with multiple coaches, organize your coaches prior to the game or season to determine which one will speak to the team. All coaches can have input, but pick the three most important or most easily correctable topics and have one coach explain them to the group. Select the most important issues, and address those. Save the rest for practice, or, if the other coaches must speak, have them talk to individuals after the group talk has been completed, just prior to the second half.

During the game and always, be sure to respond to the ideas of assistant coaches diplomatically. Their opinions are important, too. A weekly meeting or phone call with your assistants to discuss team issues can help to allow every interested and involved party to share their ideas.

Coaching points can be broken into two categories. Use reinforcement particulars to identify correct actions of individuals and groups during the game. Point out a good action that occurred to encourage others to recreate the action and to let players know that you are happy with their play. Correction ideas are used to change an action. Use correction points to identify a different response that should occur during a specific situation.

With either type of coaching point, be as specific as possible, but keep the explanation simple. When correcting, give specific information of what needs to be done to perform the action correctly.

POSTGAME

After the game is over, the players are probably going to be either ecstatic or depressed. In either case, their attention spans will not be very long, due to mental and physical fatigue. As with halftime, your approach should be organized and the time used efficiently.

Your attitude, mannerisms, and actions will play a large part in how your players leave the match. If you are a competitive person, a win or loss by your team can directly affect your emotions. There are times when showing disappointment in your players' efforts can help motivate them to perform better. Many times, however, players may react in a manner opposite of what you hoped for. Extreme criticism can turn them off and can make them lose interest in playing the game. You must recognize their efforts and be less concerned with results. Many times a hard-fought loss is a better-played game than a sloppy victory. If you find yourself to be highly emotional, compose yourself prior to addressing the team. Soccer players want to please their coaches. Their relationship with you and their perception of how you care for them as a person first and a player second are crucial.

Regardless of your message, get the team together where distractions are a minimum. If there is no game following yours, go on the field away from the bench. If you must leave the field immediately following the game, go to a place off to the side where you can gather the team around you. Try to be in a place where everyone can hear you, and explain to the parents prior to the first game that they should respect the team's privacy and stay clear of the meeting. The players' attention spans are short, so your meeting should last only a few minutes.

At the end of the game, complete these four tasks before dismissing the team:

1. Do a team cool-down
2. Assess injuries
3. Remind players of next practice
4. Use observations from the match to plan your next training sessions

After the team shakes hands with the opposition, have them do a simple cool-down that consists of light running and stretching. This is more important for players age 11 and older. The cool-down is used to prepare the body for the stoppage of activity and is the opposite of the warm-up. A cool-down should last only a few minutes and should be completed as a team.

After the cool-down, check quickly to see if anyone has suffered any injuries during the game. Keep an eye on the players but also ask them directly. If any injuries need follow-up, speak with the player's parents.

Finish the postgame meeting by mentioning the location and time of the next practice, even if it will occur at the normally scheduled time. Congratulate the team on their effort, but try not to make comments about the game. The players will be either happy or sad, and they are sure to get a synopsis of their play on the way home. Any comments that you make may be wasted. This is very important if the game was tough and you are not happy with their play. Put on a good front and bite your tongue. You do not want to say something in the heat of the moment that you will regret later.

While the game is still fresh in your mind, make some notes to plan for the upcoming practices. The notations could be about topics to work on, or they could be comments that you need to explain to the team. If you have issues about their play that you need to discuss, do it at the next training session when you will have their complete attention.

SUMMARY

Managing your team throughout the season can prove to be a challenging task, but is actually quite simple if you stay organized. Prepare for the season, but be open to change. A plan will help you stay on track and use time efficiently. People also tend to resist change, so the more routine you can make things throughout the season and at games the less chances of problems with the players.

Approach games with a sense of order, but no matter what happens, remember that the players are young children and that it is only a game. Keep your sense of humor, and do not treat the players like professionals. They play soccer because it is fun—part of your job is to make sure that it stays that way.

Appendix: Sample Training Plans

FOLLOWING ARE A FEW sample training plans that contain all the necessary ingredients for a successful session. Each plan has a theme, and includes a warm-up, a main activity, and a final game phase. In addition, each training session contains activities that are developmentally appropriate for the age groups being coached and is presented on a sample practice planning form.

Team Name: <u>U8 Sample Session</u>
Date: <u>2/1/01</u>
Theme: <u>Dribbling</u>

	Time	Exercise	Description	Coaching Points
Warm-Up	0:00–20:00	Autobahn Game Juggling with a bounce Stretching	**Autobahn Game:** All players have a ball (their car) in a 15-yard-by-15-yard grid. Players "drive" their cars without colliding with others. Calls of "Left," "Right," "U-turn," or "Brakes" result in appropriate action.	1. Introduce each change of direction separately. 2. 2 min. Autobahn, 2 min. juggling, 2 min. stretch. 3. Repeat 3 times.
Main Activities	20:00–40:00	Main Activity 1: Dinosaur Eggs Main Activity 2: Red Light/Green Light	**Dinosaur Eggs:** Players in 4 groups in a 15-yard-by-15-yard grid. Each group has a dino name and a home corner (nest). Place all balls (eggs) in center. On *Go*, all teams try to get 2 more eggs than number of players in their nest. **Red Light/Green Light:** All players with ball at start. Dribble on green, stop on red. Players moving when leader calls red must return to start.	1. Play each game for 5 minutes, repeat each twice. 2. Let players discover best ways to play. 3. Use same grid for both games.
Final Game	40:00–55:00	Game: Steal the Bacon	20-yard-by-30-yard grid with goals on each end. Divide team into 2 groups. Each player assigned a number (1, 2, . . .) so each team has one of each number. Coach calls out number and appropriate players play to goal. When ball leaves field, new number.	1. Can assign players colors or names. 2. Can call out more than one number at a time.
Cool-Down	55:00–60:00	Light jogging		

Comments about session: Keeps everyone active, simple to run, all games involve every player at all times.

Team Name: U10 Sample Session
Date: 2/1/01
Theme: Passing

	Time	Exercise	Description	Coaching Points
Warm-Up	0:00–20:00	Change Game Juggling	**Change Game:** All players with ball, dribbling in 15-yard-by-15-yard grid. When coach calls "Change" all players change direction.	1. Show different ways to change direction. 2. Work on juggling to rest (2 min. work/2 min. rest) 3. Make a game by telling players they can't use same change twice in a row.
Main Activities	20:00–40:00	Main Activity 1: Ms. Pac Man Main Activity 2: Pass and Follow	**Ms. Pac Man:** All players in 15-yard-by-15-yard grid without ball. 1 or 2 players are "it" (Ms. Pac Man). If players have a ball, and attempt to pass ball to hit others below waist. If a player gets hit, she gets a ball and becomes It. Last person to get caught wins. **Pass and Follow:** Group of 3, one ball. 2 players stand with each other; the 3rd stands 5–10 yards away. Ball starts on end with 2 players. One player passes ball to 3rd player and then follows. Repeat. Which team can make most passes without a mistake?	1. Play each game 5 minutes, repeat twice. 2. Pass and Follow is more "work" than Ms. Pac Man, so use Ms. Pac Man as a reward for hard work. 3. Vary Pass and Follow to require 1 touch or 2 touch passes.
Final Game	40:00–55:00	Game: 4 V 4 tournament, 3 passes is a goal	4 V 4 tourney on 20-yard-by-30-yard field. No goalkeeper. Teams score with either a regular goal, or by completing 3 passes.	1. Change team numbers if required. 2. Change number of passes if too easy/hard. 3. Rotate teams.
Cool-Down	55:00–60:00	Light jogging		

Comments about session: All active, minimal resets, all activities economical.

Team Name: <u>U12 Sample Session</u>
Date: <u>2/01/01</u>
Theme: <u>1 V 1 Attack</u>

	Time	Exercise	Description	Coaching Points
Warm-Up	0:00–25:00	Change of direction dribble, 2 moves, juggling, flexibility, repeat	15-yard-by-15-yard grid. All players have a ball. When coach says "Go" all players stop ball with foot. When coach says "Stop" all players dribble. Players work on scissors and double scissors when coach says "Play."	1. Introduce scissors and double scissors during different sets. 2. Cycle through 2 min. dribbling, 2 min. juggling, and 2 min. stretching 4 times.
Main Activities	25:00–50:00	Main Activity 1: Multigates Main Activity 2: 1 V 1 Gauntlet	**Multigates:** All players have a partner (opponent). 1 ball per pair. Use cones to set up 2-yard goals (gates) in random locations on field. Player with ball scores by dribbling through any gate in any direction. 1-minute game, 1-minute rests (passing with partner), repeat 5 times. **Gauntlet:** Team divided in 2. Three 10-yard-by-10-yard grids in a column. One defender in each grid. Attackers try to dribble through all 3 grids without losing ball. Each team gets 5 minutes.	**Multigates:** 1. Encourage change of direction and dribbling past player to score. 2. Keep track of who wins. Loser has a penalty (3 somersaults) **Gauntlet:** 1. Encourage scissors and double scissors to put opponent off balance. 2. Rotate defenders. 3. Have an actual goal to shoot upon at the end of the gauntlet.
Final Game	50:00–70:00	Game: Small-Sided Tournament	3 V 3 tournament in 30-yard-by-20-yard fields. Regular soccer, but team earns 3 points if they can dribble through the goal. Rotate teams and keep track of total points for all games.	1. Encourage players to take on opponents. 2. All players must bow to the team that scores the most points.
Cool-Down	70:00–75:00	Light jogging		

Comments about session: All active, minimal resets, all activities economical.

REFERENCES

AYSO Web site. "Soccer-American Youth Soccer Org. NSTC—Mission Statement," www.soccer.org/mission/mission.htm, Jan 9, 2001.

Houtkooper L. *Winning Sports Nutrition Training Manual.* Tucson: University of Arizona Cooperative Extension, 1994.

Howe, Bobby, "Let the Kids Play," *US Soccer,* Summer 1997, 18.

Manore, M. and Thompson, J. *Sport Nutrition for Health and Performance.* Champaign, IL: Human Kinetics, 2000, 417–32.

Martens, Rainer, *Successful Coaching.* Champaign, IL: Human Kinetics, 1997, 4.

Otis C. L., Drinkwater, B., Johnson, M., Loucks, A., Wilmore J. "The Female Athlete Triad." *Medicine & Science in Sports & Exercise* 29 (1997): i–ix.

GLOSSARY

Assistant referee An official positioned on the sideline who helps the referee during a match by signaling with a flag. Used to be referred to as linesmen.

Balance Defensively covering areas of the field away from the ball that attackers might try to utilize. Balance is the responsibility of the third defenders.

Combination play The coordinated action of two or more attacking players to move the ball to penetrate the defense.

Corner kick A direct kick earned by the attacking team when the defending team last touches a ball before it goes over their endline. The kick is taken from the corner nearest the point where the ball left the field.

Cover The responsibility of the defensive players who position themselves behind the first defender. The job of cover players is to pressure an attacker who dribbles past the first defender.

Curving the ball The technique of passing a ball that curves in the air. The passer strikes the ball so it has a sideways spin. Effective at getting around an object or at making a shot on goal more difficult to block.

Cut the ball The technique of using the feet when dribbling to change the direction of a ball by a sharp angle.

Defensive heading A defensive technique of using the head to get a ball away from the other team or away from a dangerous area.

Depth The distance on the field at any given time between the most forward and rearmost players on a team, not including the goalkeeper.

Direct free kick (*See* Direct kick)

Direct kick A free kick during which the attacking team may score by kicking the ball directly into the opponent's goal. The ball does not need to touch anyone but the shooter.

Double pass A combination play during which the ball carrier plays the ball to a supporting player, who immediately passes it back. The supporting player then runs past the defender and receives another pass from the ball carrier.

Double scissors A dribbling fake used to beat opponents.

Dribbling Technique of moving around the field while possessing the ball with the feet.

Driven pass Technique of passing with the instep; used to move the ball over longer distances, either on the ground or in the air.

Endline The boundaries of the field on either end. The goals are located on the endlines.

Even numbers Game situation in which there are an equal number of attackers and defenders near the ball.

Finesse finish Technique of shooting to score when very near to the goal. Emphasis is on accuracy over power. Also known as short-range finishing.

Finishing Shooting the ball to score a goal.

First defender The defensive player who is nearest to and directly responsible for defending the opponent with the ball.

Flats Flat-soled shoes with no cleats or studs.

Forward Position name of players at the front of a team whose main job is to set up and score goals. Also known as strikers.

Fullback Position name of primarily defensive players who play in front of the goalkeeper.

Goal The area bounded by two posts and a crossbar into which each team is trying to get the ball. When a ball passes into the goal, the attacking team scores.

Goal area The small box marked on the field directly in front of each goal, measuring 6 yards long and 18 yards wide. Goal kicks are taken from within the goal area.

Goal kick A restart taken by the defending team when the attacking team last touches the ball before it goes over the endline. The kick is taken from anywhere inside the goal area.

Goalkeeper The player who may use her hands while inside the penalty area to stop balls shot by the opposition from entering the goal.

Heading Technique of using the head to move the ball on the field.

Indirect kick A free kick from which a goal may only be scored if the ball touches at least two players (on any team) before it enters the goal.

Juggling Technique of repeatedly keeping the ball in the air by using various parts of the body (head, feet, thighs, chest, shoulders).

Kick-off A restart at the start of each half and after a goal has been scored. The kick-off is taken at the center of the field, and must be played forward.

Marking Defensive tactic of staying very close to an offensive player.

Midfielder Player responsible for controlling the middle of the field. Midfielders are positioned in front of the fullbacks and behind the forwards.

Molded cleats Shoes with nonremoveable molded bumps on the soles that increase traction.

Numbers-down Game situation in which there are more defenders than attackers near the ball.

Numbers-up Game situation in which there are more attackers than defenders near the ball.

Offside A foul against the attacking team that occurs when a player is in an offside position and becomes a part of the play. The player becomes a part of the play when a teammate plays the ball to them. Play is restarted with an indirect free kick at the location of the offside player.

Offside position When an attacking player is nearer to the opponent's goal than to (1) the half-line, (2) the ball, and (3) the second-to-last opponent (usually the deepest field player). A player can be in an offside position without being called offside.

One-two A combination play that is used when the supporting player is ahead of the ball. The ball carrier passes the ball to the supporting player, who returns the ball with one touch to the passer after the passer has run past a defender. Also known as the wall pass.

Overlap A combination play that occurs when the supporting player comes to help from behind the ball. The supporting player runs around and past the ball carrier, and may or may not receive a pass.

Passing Technique of moving the ball from one player to another.

Penalty box Large box marked on the field in front of each goal (18 yards long by 44 yards wide). Also known as the 18-yard box and penalty area. The goalkeeper may use her hands while inside the penalty box, and any direct free kick foul occurring against the attacking team within the box results in a penalty kick.

Penalty kick A free kick that occurs when a team commits a foul that would result in a direct free kick within its own penalty box. One player from the attacking team shoots from the penalty mark and the goal may only be defended by the goalkeeper. No one but the shooter and the goalkeeper may enter the penalty box until the ball is touched by the shooter.

Penalty mark The mark on the field 12 yards from the goal from which penalty kicks are taken.

Penetration To move the ball behind a defender while maintaining possession. Individuals or teams may penetrate.

Pickup The technique of getting the ball off the ground in order to start juggling. Hands are not used in a pickup.

Pitch The soccer field.

Punt Kicking technique used by goalkeepers to get the ball far down the field to a waiting teammate. The ball is kicked out of the hands.

Red card A disciplinary sanction that results in a player being ejected from the game. The player may not be substituted for during that game.

Referee The game official responsible for enforcing rules of the game and ensuring the safety of all participants.

Restart The action of putting the ball back into play after a stoppage of play.

Scissors Dribbling fake used to beat a defender.

Screw-ins Cleated shoes with removable and replaceable cleats.

Second defender Defensive player who is in the immediate vicinity of, but not directly pressuring, the ball. The responsibility of the second defender is to provide cover. There may be one or more second defenders at any one time.

Shielding Technique of protecting the ball with the body by standing between the defender and the ball.

Shooting Technique of attempting to score a goal with a kick.

Sidelines Lines that mark the field's boundaries on either side.

Stabbing An unsuccessful attempt to dispossess an opponent by poking a foot at the ball. Also known as diving in.

Striker (See Forward.)

Tackling Technique of dispossessing an opponent who has the ball.

Tactics Strategies and decisions used by the players and teams while playing the game of soccer.

Takeover A combination play used when the ball carrier and supporting player crisscross in front of a defender. The ball carrier either allows her teammate to take the ball, or fakes the defender and keeps the ball for herself.

Technique Skills performed with a ball while playing soccer.

Third defenders Defensive players who are away from the ball. The responsibility of the third defenders is to provide balance.

Thirds of the field The three parts of the field in relation to the goal: the defending third (nearest to the goal being defended), the middle third (between the defending and the attacking thirds), and the attacking third (nearest to the opposing team's goal). Player tactics are dependent upon the third of the field in which they are located.

Throw-in Process of putting a ball back into play when the ball goes over a sideline. A team restarts the ball when the opponents have last touched the ball before it went out of play.

Tracking A defensive movement in which the defender moves with an attacker who is making a run without the ball.

Turn the ball Turning 180 degrees while in possession with the ball. A ball control technique used by forwards and midfielders.

Wall pass (See One-two.)

Width The distance between a team's two players who are furthest apart across the field.

Yellow card A disciplinary sanction resulting in a caution for the offending player. A player receiving a second yellow card in a game automatically receives a red card.

INDEX

ABOUT THE AUTHOR

John DeWitt has extensive experience coaching soccer players at every age and level of experience. He was the head women's soccer coach at the University of New Mexico from 1996 to 2000, and was the assistant women's soccer coach there in 1995. Mr. DeWitt is a member of the National Soccer Coaches Association of America and the United States Coaches Organization, and he has earned his U.S. Soccer A License and his U.S. Soccer National Youth Diploma. He also possesses an NSCAA National Diploma. Currently, Mr. DeWitt coaches a variety of club teams in the Albuquerque, New Mexico, area, including boys' and girls' teams ranging from U9 to U19. In addition to his college and local club coaching experience, Mr. DeWitt has spent a considerable amount of time working with players of all ages, and has spent the past ten years specifically working with female athletes. He is a member of the USYSA Region IV Girls Olympic Development Program (ODP) coaching staff, and from 1996 to 1998 was the head coach of the Girls U16 ODP Regional Teams. These teams were comprised of the best U16 female soccer players from the fourteen western state soccer associations that make up the USYSA Region IV during each year. The head coaching duties included overseeing the selection of players, training the team, and coaching the team in games against other regional teams and during international competition. Mr. DeWitt had the opportunity to coach the regional teams during international tours to Germany in 1998 and 1999. In 1999, Mr. DeWitt was the assistant head coach of the Girls ODP for Region IV.

Mr. DeWitt acted as a guest observer with the gold medal–winning U.S. Women's National Team during the preparations for the 1996 Olympics in Atlanta. Mr. DeWitt is also a member of the state coaching staff for the New Mexico Youth Soccer Association. His duties include working with state ODP teams and within the coaching education program as an instructor for D and E coaching licenses and Youth Module Courses. Mr. DeWitt has spent considerable time in the New Mexico area and prior to 1995 lived in Arizona, where he worked with coaches and players of teams ranging in age from under six to adult. Mr. DeWitt has also been a contributor to the "Performance Conditioning Soccer" newsletter soccer roundtable. Mr. DeWitt has Bachelor of Science degrees in electrical engineering and computer science engineering from the University of Toledo, and has a Master's Degree in exercise science from Arizona State University. Mr. DeWitt's wife, Janice Thompson, has a Ph.D. in exercise physiology, and currently works at the University of New Mexico.